A FAITH TO LIVE BY

Kenneth D. Barney

RadiantBOOKS

Gospel Publishing House/Springfield, Mo. 65802

02-0899

© 1976 by the Gospel Publishing House
Springfield, Missouri 65802
Adapted from *Ephesians* by Kenneth D. Barney © 1961 by the
Gospel Publishing House. All rights reserved.
Library of Congress Catalog Card Number: 76-27929
ISBN 0-88243-899-9
Printed in the United States of America

A teacher's guide for individual or group study with this book is
available from the Gospel Publishing House. Order No. 32-0171

Contents

Contents

1

It's No Accident

"Paul, an apostle of Jesus Christ by the will of God, to the saints which are at Ephesus, and to the faithful in Christ Jesus: Grace be to you, and peace, from God our Father, and from the Lord Jesus Christ. Blessed be the God and Father of our Lord Jesus Christ, who hath blessed us with all spiritual blessings in heavenly places in Christ" (Ephesians 1:1-3).

That expression, *in Christ*, is one of Paul's favorites. It's what the gospel is all about. There is no salvation apart from Christ. There is no favor with God apart from Christ. There are no spiritual blessings except those we find "in Christ."

Jesus did not die on the cross to induce an unwilling God to love us. He already loved us. That's why He sent the Saviour. "God so loved . . . that he gave." He loved this lost world before Jesus ever came. But that love expressed itself fully during His stay among men.

"All spiritual blessings." What a subject! The first blessing is the new birth. No others can come until this happens. Once we are saved there is the blessed baptism in the Holy Spirit, which is promised to all believers. What about strength to overcome temptation? Isn't that a spiritual blessing? Where do we obtain grace to live victoriously in a sinful world? It's another spiritual blessing, and it has to rate high on the list.

We could keep listing more of these blessings until we ran out of words. Our victory over death and the grave is the final blessing we will receive on our way from this world to the next.

Remember that all of these reach us through Christ's mediation. He is in the presence of God praying continually for us. He knows what we need before we recognize the need ourselves. Without Him there would be no spiritual benefits at all.

These blessings come from the Father to Christ, then from Christ to us. Yes, as Christians we share what is Christ's. Jesus said to Mary Magdalene, "I ascend unto my Father, and your Father; and to my God, and your God" (John 20:17).

Notice that these blessings are spiritual. God does not promise us riches and honor on earth. We look for "a city which hath foundations, whose builder and maker is God" (Hebrews 11:10). That's far better, isn't it?

GOD THOUGHT ABOUT US LONG AGO

"According as he hath chosen us in him before the foundation of the world, that we should be holy and without blame before him in love: having predestinated us unto the adoption of children by Jesus Christ to himself, according to the good pleasure of his will, to the praise of the glory of his grace, wherein he hath made us accepted in the beloved" (Ephesians 1:4-6).

Now Paul leaps back into the remote ages of a past eternity. What he says is stupendous. God thought about us, loved us, and planned for our salvation before He ever created the universe. That's right! This was revealed to the apostle by the Holy Spirit.

The plan of salvation was not God's hasty reaction to the emergency of sin. God knew man's fall was coming before it happened. He conceived the plan of redemption before there was a man on earth.

We are treading on sacred ground here. These are realms too great for human reasoning. This is where faith enters the picture. God has done the planning and choosing. We must accept the provisions of His love.

We can't help thinking gloomily about what the devil has done to the human race. But let's never forget what God has done. He started the process of salvation before Satan began his work. God knew what the enemy was going to do before he did it. The Lord had His plan ready before Satan devised his. Isn't that wonderful!

Always remember that God's choice of us is Christ-centered. We are "chosen *in Him*." Somewhere in the eternities of the past the Father and Son made a covenant. It related to the human race which was not even created. The Father promised the blessings of His grace. The Son promised to carry out the plan that would make these blessings available to a world of lost sinners.

In Revelation 13:8 Jesus is called "the Lamb slain from the foundation of the world." He was not yet literally slain but in the mind of God He was. This shows clearly that the plan of salvation was in the thoughts of God before the dawn of Creation.

God meant to do more than save us from destruction. He wants to build in us the character of His Son. His goal is for us to be "holy and without blame." This cannot be achieved by mere human effort. It is

7

the work of the Holy Spirit in the soul. Of course, it takes our cooperation. We must be diligent in our reaching for more of God.

JESUS' BLOOD WAS REQUIRED

"In whom we have redemption through his blood, the forgiveness of sins, according to the riches of his grace" (Ephesians 1:7).

God taught the lesson of redemption throughout the Old Testament. Always it was the blood of an innocent substitute that was required. When Adam and Eve lost their innocence through sin they were ashamed to show themselves to God because they realized they were naked. Their pitiful effort to cover themselves with fig leaves is quite a picture. It symbolizes man's effort, even today, to cover his spiritual nakedness by natural means.

When God found the pair hiding in the Garden, He shed the blood of innocent animals to make coats for them. This was the first lesson about blood atonement. It was a picture of the day when Christ would shed His blood on the cross. He was sinless, but He became man's substitute. By His death man's sinful nature can be covered. Covered by what? By the righteousness of the sinless Saviour.

Every animal killed in Old Testament days pointed to the death of Jesus. Someone has well said that a scarlet line of redemption runs through the Bible from Genesis to Revelation.

Man is a sinner by nature. The Bible teaches that from the first page to the last. A sinner needs more than instruction or example. He must be liberated and cleansed. We cannot be educated out of our sin. Neither can we reason our way out. We cannot rationalize ourselves out of our guilt before a holy

God. Good resolutions and noble desires will not accomplish our deliverance. Sin has put us in a predicament that we can't get out of without help—God's help.

Jesus came to do more than improve our nature. He came to change it. Salvation gives us a new nature. Unless this change takes place there is no possibility of our inheriting everlasting life.

The gospel of Christ is a message of forgiveness. Our sins are blotted out by the precious blood of Jesus. They are buried in the sea of God's forgetfulness. He will not bring them back and accuse us after we have been pardoned.

To be redeemed is to be bought with a price. We are doubly the Lord's property when we are saved. We belonged to Him in the first place because He is our Creator. We were lost to Him through sin, but now He owns us again through the price paid by His Son. No wonder Paul talks about the "riches" of His grace. There is no way to measure this kind of riches.

YOU'RE AN HEIR

"In whom also we have obtained an inheritance, being predestinated according to the purpose of him who worketh all things after the counsel of his own will: that we should be to the praise of his glory, who first trusted in Christ" (Ephesians 1:11, 12).

What is an inheritance? It is "a possession or blessing, especially one bestowed as a gift." So says the dictionary.

This description fits our spiritual experience exactly. Our inheritance is a gift from God. It is bestowed on us through His grace. It is a result of our trusting in the blood of Christ.

9

It is impossible to describe our inheritance fully because "it doth not yet appear what we shall be" (1 John 3:2). Certainly it is beyond anything our mortal minds can conceive. Many people have a superficial idea of heaven. We are not going to spend eternity daydreaming. Idle people are not happy. In heaven we will be eternally occupied in service to God. Best of all, that service will not be limited by the kind of obstacles we have on earth.

The Bible does mention things that will *not* be present in heaven. Among them are sickness, pain, death, temptation, sin, and the presence of Satan. There will be no parting from friends and loved ones. Nothing carnal shall mar the beauty of that wonderful atmosphere. The curse produced by sin will be gone forever. Our understanding will be clear. But the best part will be the presence of our Saviour.

This present world has much beauty in spite of sin. So what will it be like where there is no sin to mar the beauty? Think of the most wonderful sight you have ever witnessed—a sunset, a snow-capped mountain, or whitecaps on the ocean. Be assured that everything in heaven will cause earth's beauties to seem as nothing.

Mysteries that perplex us here will be of no consequence in our eternal home. It is doubtful if we will even remember them. Our understanding will be vastly increased. Our comprehension of God will be unclouded. Our new knowledge will dispel error, disagreements, and ignorance. There will be holiness in heaven, for without holiness no man shall see the Lord (Hebrews 12:14). And there will be rest and satisfaction unlimited.

Yes, God has a purpose for us. We are not prisoners of chance. He is in control of everything, and for this reason we need not spend sleepless nights worrying about the outcome of the day's problems.

THE TRANSACTION IS GENUINE

"In whom ye also trusted, after that ye heard the word of truth, the gospel of your salvation: in whom also, after that ye believed, ye were sealed with that Holy Spirit of promise, which is the earnest of our inheritance until the redemption of the purchased possession, unto the praise of his glory" (Ephesians 1:13, 14).

The guarantee of our inheritance in Christ is the gift of the Holy Spirit. He constantly assures us of the reality of our heritage.

Two pictures are given here. They both show the Spirit's work in the Christian life. The first is the seal. In ancient times a seal was made of some hard substance and often set in a ring. When the seal was pressed down on a soft substance such as wax or clay, an impression was made. This was affixed to a document to show that it was authentic. The purpose was somewhat the same as for the seal of a notary public or a corporation seal today. The seal shows that the document is *bona fide* and legal, not a forgery.

By giving us His Spirit, God has declared that we are His property. He owns us. Our salvation is authenticated by the indwelling of the Spirit.

The second picture describing the Spirit's work is the "earnest." This expression is still used in the commercial world. Earnest money is a sum paid to ensure the fulfillment of a bargain. It is a pledge that more will follow. The Holy Spirit is given to the Christian as God's pledge that he has eternal life. He

11

is still in the world of mortals, but there is something better yet to come.

Notice the importance of the Scriptures in our salvation. Paul says the Ephesians were saved after hearing the Word of truth. The Spirit always works through the Word. He never does anything contradictory to the Word. When we hear the truth preached it is the Holy Spirit who takes it and applies it to our hearts. This brings conviction and then salvation. No one can be saved apart from the Word. It is the "sword of the Spirit." It is the weapon He uses to break down the resistance of the sinful heart. The Word reveals the only way to heaven.

We are "the purchased possession." Our spirits are redeemed, but our redemption will not be complete until our bodies have been delivered from the curse of death. This will take place at the Resurrection when Jesus comes back. Until that time the "earnest" assures us that this final phase of redemption is coming.

"UNTO THE PRAISE OF HIS GLORY"

We are saved to bring glory to God. When Satan caused man's fall he sought to detract from God's glory. In fact, he tried to gain it for himself. Jesus came to earth to glorify God. He saves us not only to keep us out of hell, but to tell the world of the glory of God. This is the only way the world will know about the glorious gospel.

A Christian's life should be full of praise. Even if things are not going well, his salvation from sin should bring "Hallelujahs" to his heart and lips.

When we think of heaven we visualize a place where God is continually praised. If believing hearts are to be a part of heaven, here on earth they should be full of praise. This is expressed in deeds as well as words. The life of a believer should radiate thanksgiving and joy.

The angels sang, "Glory to God in the highest," on that first Christmas Eve. They could not contain their praises because they knew the Saviour had come to earth. But angels can never know the joy of being redeemed from sin. They have not sinned, so they do not know what it is like to be lost. But we do. If beings that have never sinned praise Him without ceasing, what about those who were lost but are now part of God's family? May we never lose the wonder of our salvation. If we find ourselves taking it for granted, we had better do some hard praying until the freshness of it floods our souls again.

"Let every thing that hath breath praise the Lord. Praise ye the Lord" (Psalm 150:6)!

2
Knowing and Growing

"That the God of our Lord Jesus Christ, the Father of glory, may give unto you the spirit of wisdom and revelation in the knowledge of him: the eyes of your understanding being enlightened" (Ephesians 1:17, 18).

Paul is praying. He lets the Ephesians share in his cry to God in their behalf. He is not content that they should be spiritual babies all their lives. He wants them to grow. In these verses a prayer for their increased spiritual knowledge bursts from his heart. Doubtless this is a prayer of the Holy Spirit for all Christians.

In every believer there rests the possibility of becoming strong and mature and advancing in spiritual knowledge. This kind of progress was not only the desire of Paul, but is the longing of the Lord himself.

When Paul speaks of wisdom and revelation he is talking about the supernatural kind. No one can ever discover spiritual truth by human wisdom. His comprehension must be illuminated by the Holy Spirit. "The eyes of your understanding" actually means "the eyes of your heart." Did you know your heart has eyes? It is not enough that our intellect be enlightened. We must also have a spiritually illumined heart.

14

We can never learn enough of Christ. No matter how much we know of Him, there is still more to be learned. There is always fresh knowledge which the Spirit will give us if we will listen closely to Him.

The Christian life is a little like school. We start out in the first grade learning the simple things—the fundamentals. Reciting the ABC's may seem childish to adults, but if we did not learn them as children we would not be able to read. The Holy Spirit is the Master Teacher. Jesus said He would guide us into all truth. Some learn more rapidly than others, but the Holy Spirit is very patient.

Naturally a student cannot stop with the first or second grade and feel his education is complete. There is always more knowledge available; more realms to be explored. Even after we receive our diploma we should not stop learning. This is even truer in the spiritual realm than in the natural. We can spend all eternity learning more of Christ and never reach the limit. This is surely one of the glories of heaven—to keep on learning of Him.

Hope and Riches

"That ye may know what is the hope of his calling, and what the riches of the glory of his inheritance in the saints" (Ephesians 1:18).

Note the continued emphasis on knowledge: "That ye may know." First Paul speaks of knowing the hope of God's calling. Hope is something not yet realized, but expected. What about the world's hopes today? Pretty well shattered, aren't they? But the hope of a Christian rests upon a solid foundation. It is based on God's Word. It is founded on Christ's death, resurrection, and ascension.

There are some mysteries that will never be solved until we stand in God's presence. But as we grow in spiritual knowledge we will have a greater conception of our Christian calling and the great things that lie ahead.

Here is a Scripture passage that is frequently quoted but often misunderstood: "But as it is written, Eye hath not seen, nor ear heard, neither have entered into the heart of man, the things which God hath prepared for them that love him. But God hath revealed them unto us by his Spirit: for the Spirit searcheth all things, yea, the deep things of God" (1 Corinthians 2:9, 10).

We often stop reading this passage after "for them that love him." Some think this refers to heaven. Not so. It refers to spiritual truths that can be known now. The unconverted man cannot grasp these things with his mind. He cannot see them with his physical eyes. His heart cannot lay hold of them. But the Spirit of God teaches them to the Christian.

Why does Paul talk about riches? He was a poor man. He had very little he could call his own. But he was rich in the things that matter. Multitudes are rich in this world's goods but spiritually bankrupt. What kind of riches are you working for?

The world's riches must be left behind at death. The riches Paul is talking about will never fade. Christians are not paupers. They are not defeated. They are children of the King. They are conquerors.

What we have in Christ we did not earn. He earned it for us by His death on the cross. It is all by His grace. His atonement has provided for us everything we need for this life and the next. Any Christian who lives below his spiritual privileges is foolish indeed. Don't let the devil give you an inferiority com-

16

plex! Never feel downtrodden because the children of this present age exclude you from their company. Your riches are greater than theirs!

WHAT POWER!

"And what is the exceeding greatness of his power to us-ward who believe, according to the working of his mighty power" (Ephesians 1:19).

The word *power* stands out in this verse. This power is *in believers*. Paul longed for God's people to realize this. Think of the energy of God being actually released in us through the Holy Spirit!

This power is greater than that of Satan and the world. In our own strength we are too feeble for the conflict. Our understanding is limited. Our hearts are cold. We are like machinery that stands idle until the electric current is turned on. When it is, power is released into the working parts. Great forces are then set in motion. When we recognize the power of God that He waits to release in us, we have grasped a force that will make us spiritual giants instead of midgets.

Even the inspired mind of Paul was taxed to find words to express the staggering power of which he was writing. He speaks of "the exceeding greatness of his power." He says this power is "mighty."

We are acquainted with power in the world around us. We know what dynamite can do. We have seen great locomotives driven by steam and diesel power. Electricity to light our cities is generated by great dynamos. What about the fearsome power of a nuclear blast?

But man's greatest efforts are feeble when compared to God's power. Man can kill his millions, but only God can raise the dead. Man cannot release anyone from sin. He cannot break the power of Satan in human lives. But God can—and does.

Note the reference to God's power in Christ's ascension. As the majestic figure of the risen Lord rose from the earth, gravity's power had to yield. It was pushed aside by a greater power.

But "his power to us-ward who believe" is the most miraculous of all. That power has saved us and cleansed us from our sins. It has delivered us from spiritual darkness. It has given us the victory over the devil. It has made us more than a match for this present age with all of its devilish forces.

Believe is the key word in this verse. Faith is the switch we push to release the power of God in our lives. If you do not believe in His power you will never feel it. Doubt, fear, and skepticism will short-circuit that power in you. You will never know the thrill of being quickened by it. So let your prayer always be, "Lord, increase my faith."

ABOVE EVERY NAME

"Which he wrought in Christ, when he raised him from the dead, and set him at his own right hand in the heavenly places, far above all principality, and power, and might, and dominion, and every name that is named, not only in this world, but also in that which is to come" (Ephesians 1:20, 21).

It was power that produced the miracle of Christ's resurrection. That same power works in the hearts of believers. It is by this power that the new birth takes place, for we are "born of the Spirit." It is this power that comes upon us when we are baptized in the Holy Spirit.

18

God showed His power also when He set Christ at His own right hand after raising Him from the dead. In ancient times the place at the king's right hand was a seat of special honor and authority. Ever since His ascension Jesus has occupied such a place in heaven. His ascension proves that His work of redemption has been completed.

"Where I am, there ye may be also." This was Jesus' promise in John 14:3. We are on earth now, but this is only temporary. When we are through with earth, we shall just begin to live. Death cannot have the last word as far as Christians are concerned. They share in Christ's victory over sin, Satan, and the grave.

Christians make no pilgrimages to the grave of their Leader. He *has* no grave. The tomb in which His body temporarily lay lost its Occupant after 3 days. The Founder of our religion is at God's right hand. He has been there ever since the day the disciples saw Him disappear through the clouds. The first Christian martyr, Stephen, saw Him just before He died. Saul of Tarsus saw Him on the Damascus road. John saw Him while imprisoned on the Isle of Patmos. Above all, the coming of the Holy Spirit is our great assurance that Jesus is at the Father's right hand.

History has produced many great names. But the name of Jesus eclipses them all. It is the Name that brings salvation, peace, and deliverance.

There are names that will be prominent in the world to come—Moses, Elijah, Paul, Peter, and others. But the apostle is quick to tell us that the name of Jesus is far above them all.

Jesus' name involves His character and all that He

19

is. It speaks to us of holiness, compassion, love, wisdom, and power. It is a name that never loses its beauty and sacredness.

THE HEAD AND THE BODY

"And hath put all things under his feet, and gave him to be the head over all things to the church, which is his body, the fullness of him that filleth all in all" (Ephesians 1:22, 23).

That's as decisive as you can get: "All things under his feet." This is total victory. No enemy can stand before the power of our mighty Christ. If it seems that there are forces still rising up against Him, you can be sure that they will be put down in the end.

Christ is Lord of the Church. First, He was made Head over all things to the Church. Second, He was made the Head of the Church itself. The Church, Paul says, is His body.

How privileged the Church is to have such a Head. He holds the same relationship to the Church spiritually as the head holds to the body physically. The head directs every movement of the body. It is actually the body's life, for if the brain dies life comes to an end. The body cannot even move without directions from the head.

Isn't this a great picture? We get our directions from Christ. He is our Life. If we are cut off from Him we are doomed spiritually.

Every pain in the body is felt in the brain. Doesn't this speak of the sympathy Christ has for every bit of suffering His people endure?

Every pleasant sensation in the body is also felt in the brain. Christ shares our joys as well as our sorrows. We are vitally united with Him. We are part of Him, and He is part of us.

20

When we speak of the body of Christ we are not referring to any particular denomination. No church contains all the members of Christ's body. Those who are redeemed by the blood of Jesus are brothers and sisters spiritually regardless of their denominational affiliation. We are part of the Body through the new birth, not by religious ritual.

The Head and the Body are indispensable to each other. We know that we need Christ, but it is amazing to think that He also needs us. We were created for His fellowship. He carries out His work through His body. He can be known to the world only through the members of His body. This places our Christian life on a high plane indeed. We must be holy in word, deed, and thought.

Unconverted people cannot comprehend the closeness of Christ and His people. Only when we are in Christ through the new birth can we know and enjoy the beauty of this closeness. It is beyond all natural reasoning.

THE SCHOOL OF THE HOLY SPIRIT

The Christian life must never come to a standstill. Graduation exercises in school are called "commencement." Students who think this is the end of their learning soon find out different. They have simply been through a training period that will enable them to "commence" their quest for greater knowledge. So it is in the realm of the spiritual. Salvation and the infilling of the Spirit only prepare us for the lifelong search for more and more of Christ.

Jesus emphasized the Holy Spirit's teaching ministry. A good teacher is one who can move at the student's pace. He is willing to remain on one point as long as necessary to make sure the student learns it. We can be very thankful the Holy Spirit is such a Teacher. If He despaired of our dullness and gave up on us we would be finished!

We must sharpen our spiritual sensitivity to the Spirit's leading. If we are to know more of Christ it will be through the Spirit's great teaching ministry. If we grow to spiritual maturity it will be because of the Spirit's life within us.

Regular prayer habits must be established. Regular Bible study is a "must." Faithful worship in God's house must be a part of every week's schedule.

We cannot get along on yesterday's meals physically. Neither can we make it on last Sunday's spiritual blessings. We must be "anointed with *fresh* oil." This needs to happen every day. If we neglect our private daily devotions our knowing and growing will lag badly.

The real fruit of the Spirit is Christian character. As we move along in His school that fruit will appear. No amount of activity is a substitute for that fruit. Only as we become Christlike can we know more of Him.

It is sad to get a taste of God's power and never go on to find out what it is really like to move ahead in the Christian life. First become grounded in the fundamentals of the Christian life. Don't try to launch out into deep things until you know your ABC's. Rely heavily on your Teacher. He will take you on and on and on. If there is any stopping place it's your fault, not His.

3

It's Different Now

"And you hath he quickened, who were dead in trespasses and sins" (Ephesians 2:1).

To *quicken* means to bring to life. That's what really happens in salvation.

Death isn't pleasant to think about. Heartache and tears, separation and loss are associated with death. It is something we don't like to talk about. Yet it is universal. It invades the palace and the hut. It strikes the old and the young.

But Paul is writing about spiritual death. This is the condition of all who are not saved. They are dead!

We were dead in trespasses and sins, Paul declares. Spiritual death made us unresponsive to God. We had no communion with Him. Our life was pointed in the wrong direction. We served the devil instead of the Lord. That's spiritual death!

The spiritually dead often fail to recognize their true condition. They may join a church and do good deeds thinking this will give them divine favor. But no amount of good works can raise the dead. Only God can do it through Christ. The dead cannot raise themselves. They cannot raise one another. Either they turn to the Lord for help or they stay in the grave of sin.

Everyone who is now saved was once a spiritual corpse. Sometimes it's good to remember what we were before we found Christ. We must never lose the wonder of our salvation. Let's never take it for granted.

We think of the raising of the dead as a miracle. It is. The raising of the spiritually dead is the greatest miracle of all.

Unsaved people do not understand the deadly power of sin. Many treat it lightly. They make jokes about it. Something that kills isn't funny!

Spiritual death is not a future state. It is present now in the life of the sinner. If he dies without Christ that death will continue throughout eternity. It will result finally in what the Bible calls "the second death."

"You hath he quickened." This is the miracle of the gospel. God, through Christ, has brought us to life. No wonder we get excited about our salvation—we're celebrating a resurrection! We have left the grave behind. Every day for us is now a new day of life.

SLAVES TO A PRINCE

"Wherein in time past ye walked according to the course of this world, according to the prince of the power of the air, the spirit that now worketh in the children of disobedience: among whom also we all had our conversation in times past in the lusts of our flesh, fulfilling the desires of the flesh and of the mind; and were by nature the children of wrath, even as others" (Ephesians 2:2, 3).

What was our *walk* before we were Christians? It was "according to the course of this world," Paul says. We copied the rest of the devil's crowd. We

24

were led by the spirit of the age. We were in the broad way that leads to destruction, and we lived like it.

"The prince of the power of the air" is, of course, Satan. In 2 Corinthians 4:4 he is called "the god of this world." That means he is the governing force in the lives of those outside of Christ. Associating Satan with the air would seem to indicate that evil spirits have their abode in the atmosphere. They certainly exercise a real influence on human beings on earth. We see this every day.

Those who are slaves to this prince live only for the present. They give little if any thought to eternity. They make no preparations for the next world.

Notice that word *worketh*. There is a satanic activity in the life of the sinner of which he is unaware. There are many terrible deeds committed by men that can have no other explanation than the fact that they are under the control of an evil supernatural power.

Many of the devil's slaves are, of course, "respectable" sinners. They are refined and cultured. They are tragically trapped by their own morality, which blinds them to their need of Christ. They are as lost as those who live in terrible outward degradation.

Sin is universal. "We all" were Satan's slaves, the apostle wrote. We didn't simply stumble into sin occasionally. We did everything possible to satisfy our carnal nature. This made us what Paul calls "the children of wrath." We were unaware of it, but the wrath of God hung over our heads like a sword of Damocles, suspended by a slender thread called "life."

The driving force behind the sinful life is "the

25

lusts of our flesh." This covers a wide area. Paul summarizes these lusts in Galatians 5:19-21: "Adultery, fornication, uncleanness, lasciviousness, idolatry, witchcraft, hatred, variance, emulations, wrath, strife, seditions, heresies, envyings, murders, drunkenness, revelings, and such like." Not a pretty picture, is it? But it is God's description of the sinful nature.

RESCUED BY LOVE

"But God, who is rich in mercy, for his great love wherewith he loved us" (Ephesians 2:4).

God's love for sinners is the most amazing fact in the universe. When man was rushing toward inevitable ruin the love of God erected a barrier. It was the cross of Christ. If anyone loses his soul he must first smash this barrier down and go on in spite of it.

It is easy to think of someone being rich in gold or silver. But Paul says God is rich in mercy. That mercy is not a trickle. It is a mighty river. It is wide enough and deep enough to cover the whole world. It would save the entire race if men would only respond to God's voice.

Mercy is love in action. We may feel compassion for someone, yet do nothing about it. Mercy prompts us to do more than feel—it makes us act. God's love moved Him to give His only begotten Son for the sins of the world. Where would we be without God's mercy? Lost forever, of course.

In 2 Corinthians 1:3 Paul calls God "the Father of mercies." Micah 7:18 declares that "he delighteth in mercy." We are told in 1 Peter 1:3 that we are born again "according to his abundant mercy." If anyone is lost it is not because there is any shortage of mercy on God's part. He is lost in spite of it.

Anyone can love someone who is lovable. But loving the other kind is something else. God loves the worst and the vilest as well as those whom society considers respectable. He loved us when we deliberately disobeyed Him and broke His laws. In spite of our repeated rejections of His mercy He kept on loving us. How glad we can be that God did not abandon us the first time we said "No" to Him.

There is only one reason that judgment has not already fallen on this wicked human race of ours: God's mercy has held it back. He is giving men an opportunity to be saved before the stroke falls.

People sometimes wonder what we will do in heaven. Surely it will take the ages of eternity to comprehend God's love fully. It is a mystery that will keep unfolding to us.

Mercy cannot be associated with softness. It takes greatness to be merciful. It is natural to strike back and seek revenge.

Every drop of blood that dropped from Jesus' cross was literally a drop of mercy. It cost Him agonizing hours of separation from the presence of His Father, but He did not shrink from it. He suffered as a lost soul suffers to bring His Father's mercy to us.

HEAVENLY PLACES

"Even when we were dead in sins, hath quickened us together with Christ, (by grace ye are saved;) and hath raised us up together, and made us sit together in heavenly places in Christ Jesus" (Ephesians 2:5, 6).

Listen to those words again: "Even when we were dead." God started to influence us while we were still wallowing in sin. He sent the Holy Spirit to convict us of our sins. He spoke to us in countless ways even when we refused to hear Him.

Our life is different since our spiritual resurrection. We have a new walk. We live in a different atmosphere. Paul calls it "heavenly places." This means places where heaven's privileges and blessings are dispensed. It is where the air of heaven is breathed. The believer lives in an atmosphere where he feels as though heaven has already begun.

What a difference there is between a dead man and a living one. It takes several pallbearers to carry the dead, but a live man can walk by himself. He can even carry someone else.

Paul speaks not only of our spiritual resurrection, but also of our ascension. This is symbolic language, of course. When Christ ascended literally He returned to His former exalted position in heaven. Christians have an exalted position spiritually. They are victors over the world, the flesh, and the devil. They are identified with Christ in His complete victory. The Christian can rise above the foes that once defeated him.

Once we have been saved we are united with Christ. With Him we fight the battle against sin. It is no longer a matter of walking alone and doing the best we can. We walk with Christ, and His victory is ours.

One raised from the dead would not linger in the cemetery. Lazarus didn't. Certainly he didn't keep the grave clothes and fondle them tenderly. The one who has been resurrected from sin gets as far away from the old life as possible. He does not cling to old habits. He wants no part of anything that reminds him of his former spiritual death.

Note how Paul interjects the reminder, "By grace

28

ye are saved." This was the theme of his ministry. He had been a moral, upright keeper of Moses' law. He was what the world calls "a good man." But none of it saved him. Only when he recognized his lost condition and found Christ by grace did salvation flood his soul. We cannot boast of our spiritual position. We did not earn it. Grace—God's unmerited favor—is responsible for every blessing that comes our way.

THERE'S GLORY AHEAD

"That in the ages to come he might show the exceeding riches of his grace, in his kindness toward us, through Christ Jesus" (Ephesians 2:7).

What a wonderful future awaits the Christian! Life isn't long at best. But for "ages to come" the believer will be in the presence of his Lord. It will take all those ages to tell the whole story of His love.

Heaven will not be a place of inevitable boredom. We will serve the Lord there just as we do here. We will praise Him. We will be occupied with His worship.

Angels are waiting for the day when all of God's children are finally home. Are they rehearsing some special songs for that hour? Perhaps so. But Christians have a song that even angels cannot sing. They will have to listen while the redeemed sing of the Blood that washed them from their sins.

Paul uses strong language. He speaks of "the exceeding riches of his grace." That's putting it mildly, of course. But there are no words that can really describe the glories of our salvation.

With our limited human understanding we can comprehend only a little of the glory of the gospel. It will be different in heaven. Earthly limitations will be gone, and we will be constantly learning new things about our Lord. We will need glorified minds and bodies for that experience. From one age to another the picture will keep unfolding.

Notice Paul's expression, "his kindness toward us." There is an infinite sweetness about the grace of God. Grace is just what Paul says—undeserved kindness. If we could work our way to heaven God would not have to spend ages showing us the wonders of His grace. But we can't, so it has to be through grace.

How often when we are enjoying something on earth we have to stop because our "time is up." But in "the ages to come" we will be free from the bondage of time. We won't have to watch the clock or the calendar. The glory will never end! And it is all because of Jesus. His love did it. His death, resurrection, and ascension guarantee heaven for us.

RESURRECTION TAKES POWER

Man can generate enough power to blast a missile into space. He can unleash the power of the atom. But he cannot raise the dead. God's greatest display of power was not in Creation. It was when He raised His Son from the dead. That was divine power at its highest intensity.

Spiritual resurrection takes power, too. Remember how many times you promised yourself you were going to do better? How many times did you fail? How many resolutions did you break? You were trying to change yourself by your own power, but you didn't have enough.

When God came on the scene it was different. He had the power to raise you from spiritual death, and He did it when you turned to Christ in repentance. Satan's hold on a sinner's life can only be broken

30

by a power greater than his. Man's certainly isn't. How the devil must laugh at the puny efforts of humans to free themselves from his clutches. Only the power of God can lift a lost soul out of his grave.

This power begins when the Word of God finds lodging in the heart. The Holy Spirit starts the Word working. It gets into the conscience. A sense of sinfulness begins to be felt. Conviction settles down over the soul of the sinner. If he responds by yielding to the Lord the power of spiritual resurrection goes into operation. It is a miracle from first to last.

This power is available to "whosoever will." How wonderful that God has no favorites. The thief on the cross died physically, but he was resurrected spiritually. Even physical death has no real sting for the Christian. The *real* death is what comes after the death of the body if one has not accepted Christ. Salvation nullifies that. There is no second death for the believer.

The same power that raised Christ from the dead lifts the sinner out of his sins. That same power keeps him from day to day. It enables him to live victoriously in a world where sin runs rampant.

4

Amazing, Isn't It?

"For by grace are ye saved through faith; and that not of yourselves: it is the gift of God" (Ephesians 2:8).

Amazing, isn't it? The grace of God, that is. *Grace* comes from the same Latin word as "gratis," which means "without charge; out of favor or kindness."

We do not deserve salvation. We deserve judgment because of our sin. But God so loved the world that He made provision for everyone to be saved. Not all *are* saved, of course, but that's because of their own refusal to accept Christ.

When a businessman allows someone extra time for the payment of his bill it is called a period of "grace." The man doesn't have to allow it. He does it out of the goodness of his heart. It's the same with God's grace.

Man is a proud creature. He would like to boast of earning his salvation. That's why God devised a plan of salvation that wouldn't let man earn his way to heaven. The carnal nature likes to "do." But the gospel says, "The only thing you can 'do' is believe on the Lord Jesus Christ."

True Christianity sweeps aside all of man's puny efforts to save himself. It eliminates the possibility of many "ways" of salvation. There is only one way.

Jesus did not say, "I am one of the ways." He declared: "I am *the* way."

God's grace is already provided. What *we* must provide is the faith to receive it. Faith is the hand that reaches out to take the gift. Faith is not just a mental assent to the truth. It is the opening of the heart to God. It is complete trust and surrender. The human heart is like a closed door, but the Lord longs to enter it. Faith alone can open it. When faith flings open wide the door, the grace of God flows in like a healing stream.

All of God's best things are gifts. We do not earn the sunshine, the rain, or even the air we breathe. These are God's gifts. Salvation is the greatest gift of all. We cannot earn it any more than we can earn the sunlight that streams down to earth every day. "Not of yourselves, " the Word says. And we can thank God that this is true.

Grace speaks of a God who is mighty, yet gentle and loving. Jesus loved to call Him "Father."

BRAGGART, BE QUIET!

"Not of works, lest any man should boast" (Ephesians 2:9).

Paul speaks from experience. There was a day when he boasted of his spirituality. He was proud of being very religious. But none of it saved him. Only when he found Christ did he enjoy pardon from his sin. From then on he declared that the only boasting he would do would be in the Cross.

A member of the first family on earth tried to be saved by works. His name was Cain. Instead of bringing an animal and sacrificing it he brought some of the crops he had raised. Thus he was rejecting the idea of a blood sacrifice. And God rejected *him!*

Cain's brother, Abel, brought the right kind of sacrifice. It was a lamb that he killed. That lamb became his substitute. Symbolically it bore his sin. This is the basis of atonement. It is the only way God can pardon a sinner. Abel found favor with God. His slain lamb was the means of his reconciliation with the Lord.

Listen to Jesus' words in Matthew 7:22, 23: "Many will say to me in that day, Lord, Lord, have we not prophesied in thy name? and in thy name have cast out devils? and in thy name done many wonderful works? And then will I profess unto them, I never knew you: depart from me, ye that work iniquity."

This is a glimpse of the coming day of judgment. Listen to them brag about their works! And hear the Lord's stern words of rebuke. He disowns them. They have tried to work their way into heaven, and they have failed. So will everyone else.

Simon, the sorcerer of Samaria, wanted to buy the power of conveying the gift of the Holy Spirit to people (Acts 8:18, 19). Of course, he could not. But people still make the same mistake. They imagine that God can somehow be bribed into looking favorably on them because of all the good things they have done.

Some people asked Jesus, "What shall we do, that we might work the works of God?" (John 6:28). Jesus answered: "This is the work of God, that ye believe on him whom he hath sent" (v. 29). The only thing God is looking for, He declared, is faith in His Son.

The Holy Spirit, through Paul's pen, knocks out every prop from under people who trust in works. This does not set well with self-righteous folks, but

God is not trying to *please* man. He is trying to *save* him. It is tragic when religious leaders try to sugarcoat the gospel. The message is, always has been, and always will be: By grace, through faith, plus nothing.

GOD AT WORK IN MAN

"For we are his workmanship, created in Christ Jesus unto good works, which God hath before ordained that we should walk in them" (Ephesians 2:10).

Salvation is only the beginning of a brand-new life. Good works do not save us, but good works should naturally follow our conversion. This is why God redeems us—to glorify Him by the kind of lives we live. This is the only way the world can know about the power of God to save.

In this verse Paul says that in eternity God will exhibit believers as specimens of His workmanship (see verse 7). The material He has had to work with has not always been the best, has it? The lives He has taken over have often been battered and buffeted by sin. But how wonderfully He reshapes and remolds them. We couldn't straighten ourselves out, but He does the straightening so beautifully. What we are is all by His grace. We can take credit for none of it.

People who are not Christians may have what the Bible calls "a form of godliness." It is not acceptable to God, of course. Only the indwelling Holy Spirit can produce the kind of righteousness God can accept.

Good works are not something the Christian is to indulge in occasionally. They are to be a way of life. It should be as natural for a Christian to be righteous as it is for an apple tree to bear apples.

35

If we compared the Christian life to a tree we could say that grace is the root and good works are the fruit. If good works are not seen there is serious doubt that a real experience of salvation has ever occurred. If there is no fruit it is natural to question whether there is any root.

Paul puts the whole plan of salvation in a nutshell when he says we are saved by grace, through faith, unto good works. God's grace is free, but this does not mean it costs nothing to live the Christian life. We have a responsibility to live by God's laws and to do what is pleasing to Him. The Lord has standards for Christian living. He does not intend that we should experience His grace and then drop back into our old ways.

We should "walk" in good works, Paul says. The Bible often describes the Christian life as a walk. We walk a step at a time. This is how we travel from place to place. Every step a Christian takes should be a step of righteousness. Our walk should be perfectly straight, never crooked. Enoch walked with God in those terrible days before the Flood, and God's grace will keep His children today.

THE BLOOD HAS BROUGHT US CLOSE

"But now, in Christ Jesus, ye who sometime were far off are made nigh by the blood of Christ" (Ephesians 2:13).

"Far off . . . nigh." These expressions describe the past and present. What a distance there was between God and us when we were in sin. Like the Prodigal Son, we lived in the "far country."

But it's different now. Through the blood of Jesus we have been brought into God's very presence. The unconverted man cannot come close to God. He cannot understand the things that are spiritual. He is too far away. He is in a different world. With the believer things are completely revolutionized. Now he can call God his Father. His spiritual knowledge increases daily as he walks with the Lord.

All of man's misery stems from his being far from God. This applies to individuals, to nations, and to the world.

Many sincere people are working to eliminate things from our society that are unpleasant. This includes poverty, war, drugs, divorce, drunkenness, and a host of other evils. But no amount of legislation or social work will get the job done. These things exist because man has put such a distance between himself and his Maker.

Righteousness cannot be legislated. It must start in the heart. Sin starts on the inside of man. The heart must be cleansed. And it can only be cleansed by the blood of Jesus Christ.

Nobody needs to be kept away from God now. Jesus died to bring us close. Only those who deliberately reject Him are still far away.

Real nearness is a thing of the heart. Two people may be closely associated physically and yet be far apart. They may share none of the same interests or desires. When we are brought close to the Lord it is our heart that must be dealt with. We can go to church and pay lip service to the Lord without the inside of us being moved at all.

Thank God, as Christians we can use the word *sometime* in referring to being far from God. Things have changed. The past is behind. It is covered by the Blood. The record is clean.

It is easy to think of people who live degraded

lives as being far from God. The truth is that the "good moral man" without Christ is just as far away. There are many things to defile the life, but the one damning sin is rejection of Christ. Other sins are simply by-products of this one.

PEACE THAT LASTS

"For he is our peace, who hath made both one, and hath broken down the middle wall of partition between us; . . . and came and preached peace to you which were afar off, and to them that were nigh" (Ephesians 2:14, 17).

Christ is the One who established peace between the believer and God. He is the One who will maintain that peace.

The *both* in this passage refers to Jew and Gentile. The "middle wall of partition" was the law of Moses. Jesus has destroyed that barrier which kept Jews and Gentiles apart. He has made peace between them. When both accept Christ they become brothers.

"You which were afar off"—that's the Gentiles. "Them that were nigh" means the Jews, to whom God had given the Law and the covenants.

Peace is a big subject today. It is much on men's minds. Unfortunately, man doesn't have the key to it. Men cannot be at peace with each other as long as they are at war with God. That war stops when Jesus comes into the heart—and *only* then.

Peace is the absence of conflict. A man's life will be a battleground as long as he is away from the Lord. When he is reconciled to God through Christ, real peace settles down over his life.

The Bible calls Jesus the Prince of Peace. He told His disciples: "Peace I leave with you, my peace I give unto you: not as the world giveth, give I unto you. Let not your heart be troubled, neither let it be afraid" (John 14:27).

That peace was made possible through the Cross. The Bible knows nothing of a gospel without the Cross. It knows nothing of a relationship with God that is not based on the blood atonement of Jesus Christ. Remove the Cross from Christianity and you have taken away the peace treaty between God and sinners.

The angels sang of peace at Jesus' birth. Christ came from heaven with a covenant of peace for "whosoever will." One fruit of the Spirit is peace. There is no restriction on the message of peace. It is for all.

There is a false peace that is temporary. It lasts while circumstances are favorable, then it disappears. The peace Christ gives is ours when things are bad. It lasts through the storms of life. It is not a human product and cannot be destroyed by human means. In our weakness we do not always take advantage of Christ's peace, but it is there for us. It is not God's will for us to live in turmoil.

FORGET IT!

Try to save yourself? Try to make peace with God by your own merits? Forget it! You're wasting your time. You're risking the eternal welfare of your soul.

Salvation by grace alone was the theme of Paul's life and ministry. He contended for it fiercely. He preached it everywhere he went. He would not yield an inch to those who tried to be saved by works. He was often opposed by people who taught that men still had to keep the law of Moses. He declared that the Law was good, but had served its purpose. It showed men their sinfulness and prepared the way for the message of grace.

Again and again in Paul's letters he hammers on the theme of salvation by grace apart from works. No one should know better than he. He was raised in a religion of good works. He could truthfully say that he had kept the Law. He was a religious man. But he was not saved. He never knew the peace of God until he met the risen Christ on the Damascus road.

Paul refused to boast about his former religious works. In fact, he considered them nothing but trash to be thrown away and forgotten. There are many people today who need this message. They imagine that having their name on the church roster will save them. They are sure their contributions to charity and their social work will pile up points in heaven. What a tragic delusion!

One of the best-loved hymns of the church is "Amazing Grace." If salvation were by works this song would have no meaning. In fact, it would never have been written. It is nothing less than amazing that God loved us enough to save us just out of His own kindness and mercy.

As long as there are human beings there will be people, like those in Paul's day, who want to save themselves by good deeds. It makes them feel good to be doing things they imagine will bring God's smile. Of course, they don't get their teaching from the Bible.

When God's people reach their heavenly home they will sing of the One who washed them from their sins in His own blood. There will be no songs about what they did. Their works will not have gotten them there—Jesus will have!

5
Strangers No More

"For through him we both have access by one Spirit unto the Father" (Ephesians 2:18).

Men of the Old Testament knew nothing of direct access to God. The door was closed. A priest always stood to mediate between God and the sinner.

Now a human priest is not needed. We need only one priest, and we have Him. He is our great High Priest, Jesus Christ.

One of the great blessings of the gospel is access to God. Before Jesus died and rose again God had to keep man at a distance. This was because of sin. The Law could not remove sin. It only provided temporary relief from the dread disease.

Now that Jesus has died and risen again all who will believe on Him can be reconciled to God. Reconciliation means access. God and the believer are not strangers.

When we come to God it is not to a stern judge or harsh dictator. We come to a loving Father. He is merciful to those who trust in Him. He is tender toward us, even with our faults and shortcomings.

Note Paul's expression, "by one Spirit." Christ is the open Door into the Father's presence. But it is the Holy Spirit who must lead us through that door. First He convicts us of sin. Then when we repent and believe, He brings to pass in us the new birth. He applies the blood of Jesus to our guilty hearts. Thus we are cleansed and ready for an audience with God.

The Holy Spirit gives us continuing access to God all the days of our Christian life. The Spirit baptizes us into the body of Christ. His indwelling is necessary if we are to have an unbroken relationship with our Father.

In a bank only certain individuals have access to the vault where the money is kept. No one but those trusted people know the combination. To others the door is closed. Before Jesus died and rose again the great wealth of God's grace lay behind a closed door. Sin had shut it tight. But now, through Christ, the door is opened. We are no longer on the outside wishing we could get in. We have access to the limitless grace of God. Each day we discover new wonders. The Spirit of God is always showing us new spiritual treasures. There is never a dull moment!

In the Family Now

"Now therefore ye are no more strangers and foreigners, but fellow citizens with the saints, and of the household of God" (Ephesians 2:19).

Have you ever been in a foreign land? It's an uncomfortable feeling to be some place where you are a stranger. You can't read the signs. You are unable to converse with the people. Everything is unfamiliar. Sometimes there is a sense of fear and uncertainty. As a foreigner you don't have the privileges citizens enjoy.

Sin makes men strangers and foreigners to God. The sinner is not comfortable in a spiritual atmosphere. The words of the Bible are a foreign language to him. He is ill at ease in the presence those who speak the language of the Spirit.

But salvation brings a glorious change. The Christian is a citizen of God's kingdom, with all the privileges thereof. He is not only a citizen of the Kingdom, but a member of God's family. He enters a new fellowship. The things of God are no longer an enigma. The Bible becomes an open book.

No human relationship is sweeter than that of the family. Folks in the same household share secrets not divulged to others. They know each other intimately. The sorrows and joys of one are shared by all.

But the bond that unites Christians is even stronger than a blood relationship. There is nothing on earth to compare with the thrill of being part of God's family.

Sinners live in the world God created, but they cannot fellowship with the Creator. Their names are not written in heaven. As far as the kingdom of God is concerned they are just what Paul says: "Strangers and foreigners."

The Christian is not a casual visitor to God's household. He is part of the family. This is a privilege not to be treated lightly.

Our relationship to God through Christ is everlasting. It is indestructible. Christ did not reconcile us to His Father for a day, but forever. So strong is our relationship with God that Paul exclaims in Romans 8:38, 39: "For I am persuaded, that neither death, nor life, nor angels, nor principalities, nor powers, nor things present, nor things to come, nor height, nor depth, nor any other creature, shall be able to separate us from the love of God, which is in Christ Jesus our Lord."

A powerful promise, isn't it? God has not only provided a home in heaven for us, but He watches over us so that we will arrive there safely!

An Unshakable Foundation

"And are built upon the foundation of the apostles and prophets, Jesus Christ himself being the chief corner stone" (Ephesians 2:20).

In a material temple the stones are dead material. In God's spiritual temple, the Church, the stones are living. They are human beings who have been redeemed by Jesus' blood.

Man builds his temple of the materials of earth. God builds His of never-dying souls.

The foundation of the Temple has already been laid. It is the gospel as preached by the apostles and prophets. No man dares lay another.

Don't forget the cornerstone. It determines the lines of the whole building. It regulates the shape of the foundation. We do not determine the pattern of the Church. The Lord Jesus Christ, the chief Cornerstone, has already done so. It is to the extent that we conform to His pattern that we shall be successful. To deviate from it only invites chaos and confusion.

A building can be no stronger than its foundation. A religion whose foundation is only the opinions of men will not stand. Paul was one who helped lay the Church's foundation. He described it in 1 Corinthians 15:3, 4: "For I delivered unto you first of all that which I also received, how that Christ died for our sins according to the Scriptures; and that he was buried, and that he rose again the third day according to the Scriptures." That's the Church's foundation.

A foundation is for support. It must be strong enough to bear a tremendous weight over a long period of time. It is subject to great stress and strain.

In a building program nothing receives more attention than the pouring of the foundation. If a mistake is made here the whole building will be adversely affected. Thank God, the Church has a foundation that will never crack! It will not shift—it will remain as long as the Church is on earth.

Apostasy and false doctrine have been introduced into the Church from time to time, but still the foundation stands. Persecutors have beat fiercely against the walls of the Church, but still the foundation remains. It bears up the great weight resting on it.

Be sure your faith as a Christian is based "on nothing less than Jesus' blood and righteousness," as the old hymn declares. Never try to lean on someone else's experience. Do not depend on your changeable feelings and emotions. They are affected by too many things. The Biblical foundation is the only safe one.

FITLY FRAMED AND GROWING

"In whom all the building fitly framed together groweth unto a holy temple in the Lord" (Ephesians 2:21).

God does not have many temples. Only one. "Fitly framed together" is a beautiful way of describing the Church's unity. We are members of one another. Each member is needed. If one stone falls out of a wall a gap is left that is noticeable. The same is true of the Church.

Let each stone be content in its own place and never desire to be elsewhere. The Holy Spirit knows just where each one belongs. He shapes it to fit the exact position where He wants it. Not all of us have the same ability, talent, or ministry. Some stones fit where others do not. We must leave all of this to the Master Designer.

Each stone in a building receives stability and strength from those it rests against. Each stone gets and gives support. Each one is essential to the design and symmetry of the whole structure. It is sad when a disgruntled Christian complains, "I'm not needed. No one would miss me if I left the church." It isn't so!

The ministry of every member of the church is for the edification of the whole. Each of us should seek conscientiously to fill the place where God puts us. We are not serving ourselves, but the whole Church.

Paul says this Temple is growing. It is not completed yet, but day by day it is "growing." A church that is not growing is dead. It is possible to grow in numbers but not in spirituality. There should be an increase in both areas.

The Early Church had few material advantages. They usually met in the homes of believers, since they had no established church buildings. Yet the church grew by leaps and bounds. We must never forget that the progress of the church is dependent on the efforts of each individual. If just one is letting down on the job it will slow down the whole body. God wants His temple to be growing constantly.

Being "fitly framed together" indicates our nearness to one another. We are not isolated individuals. We are members of a Body. We are part of a spiritual Temple.

We should not fail to note the qualifying phrase, "in the Lord." A church can engage in many efforts that are not "in the Lord." Carnality can get the upper hand if every Christian does not diligently guard against it.

"In whom ye also are builded together for a habitation of God through the Spirit" (Ephesians 2:22).

A *habitation* is a place to live. Christians are intended to be God's home. Could there be a greater incentive to holy living? Let's be sure His home is always clean.

The Old Testament temple was a building wholly dedicated to God. The Church must be the same. It is terrible to defile it by allowing sin, false doctrine, and discord to enter. The Church is God's home, but He cannot live where there is rubbish and filth.

All too often revival among the unsaved has been hindered because the Church has lost its separation from the world. The Church is not merely a religious organization. It is the temple of the living God.

Every heathen temple was built as a home for some false god. The true Church is the dwelling place of the God of heaven. He does not live in man-made temples. It is the spirit of the true believer that becomes His temple. Collectively, all Christians form the spiritual temple that is the Church.

If you live in a house very long you become a part of it. It is hard to leave a place where you have lived for many years. A strange unity develops between you and that house, even though it is inanimate. How much more does the Lord become a part of the Temple where He dwells. And the Temple becomes a part of Him.

What an amazing relationship there is between the Lord and His church. This should make us walk very carefully before Him. We should delight to keep God's home in order.

The temples built by men are going to decay and fall someday. But God's true temple is indestructible. It survives wars, persecutions, apostasy, and all of the attacks of evil. The death of believers does not affect the progress of the Church. Part of the Temple is on earth; the greater part is in heaven. But one day God will gather all the stones together.

The true glory of the Church is not outward beauty, but the presence of God. Let us walk softly in the light of that great truth.

Again, we have a qualifying phrase, "through the Spirit." The Holy Spirit is the great Overseer of God's building program on earth. The blueprint is the Bible. Nothing the Spirit ever does will deviate from the blueprint. When we do, God's work suffers. Only as we operate within divine guidelines can we expect divine blessing. The Spirit is building the Church, and He discards the material that is carnal.

NOW WE KNOW WHO WE ARE

Much has been said in recent years about an "identity crisis" suffered by many people. Some have declared that rioting and unrest are produced by those who cannot identify with anything. It has been said by some that restless youth are simply trying to find out who they really are.

There is no such problem for the Christian. He knows who he is, where he came from, and where he is going. He is God's property. He has been redeemed by the blood of His Son. He has an open door into his Father's presence. He belongs to the heavenly family. He is the home of the Holy Spirit. He stands on a foundation that is solid. No wonder the Christian can survive the stress and strain that others cannot.

The best part of all is that there is no end to the thrills of the Christian life. Salvation is just the beginning. Everyday we learn a little more about our position in Christ. With the help of the Holy Spirit we delve a little deeper into His unsearchable riches.

Pity the man who thinks he is only a higher animal. The Christian knows he is more than the product of some vague evolutionary process. He was created by the hand of God, and then he was bought back from sin by the precious blood of God's Son. Now he is a child of the King.

Man-made religion tries to humanize God; to bring Him down to man's level. This is foreign to the teaching of the Bible. The gospel lifts man up to God's level. It elevates his life in every area. It sets him "in heavenly places."

If we are members of God's family we should act like it. There is no reason to live in fear and panic. Christ has made His peace available to us. He assures us of our Father's care. He encourages us to eliminate fear from our thinking.

A sense of "belonging" is essential to our well-being. To be a "loner" is a miserable existence. It is a part of the glory of the gospel to know that we are not alone. We are part of God and He is part of us. We have a place to fill in His church. We are needed. God himself longs for our fellowship. Such a thought ought to keep us going in the most trying days.

6

A Secret No Longer

"How that by revelation he made known unto me the mystery; (as I wrote afore in few words; whereby, when ye read, ye may understand my knowledge in the mystery of Christ,) which in other ages was not made known unto the sons of men, as it is now revealed unto his holy apostles and prophets by the Spirit; that the Gentiles should be fellow heirs, and of the same body, and partakers of his promise in Christ by the gospel" (Ephesians 3:3-6).

In the scriptural sense a mystery is a truth known only by divine revelation. God chose to reveal a number of mysteries to Paul. One of these was the mystery of the Church.

By the "Church" we mean the called-out body of believers from Pentecost to the Rapture. The most significant aspect of the mystery as far as the Jews were concerned was this: the Church would be composed of both Jews and Gentiles. They would become one in Christ.

The long-standing prejudice against Gentiles did not melt away overnight. Even Jews who were Christians had difficulty believing that Gentiles could be saved without keeping the Law. In fact, the church almost split over this matter (Acts 15).

Paul's preaching of salvation by grace through faith apart from works did much to hasten the breakdown of these prejudices. Paul made it clear that he spoke with the authority of heaven behind him. He had a revelation from God. What had been a mystery was made known to this chosen apostle. He, in turn, made it known to the church.

Paul did not stumble on this truth accidentally. It was a direct revelation from the Holy Spirit. Paul disclaimed any credit for his understanding. He had not grasped the truth intellectually. It was a revelation from heaven.

The word *church* does not appear in the Bible until Jesus declared, "Upon this rock I will build my church" (Matthew 16:18). Pentecost was the day the Church was born. It will not be completed until Jesus comes again.

Other New Testament leaders received the revelation about the Church, but Paul was its chief exponent. Others came to understand it more gradually. Peter probably understood it after his visit to Cornelius' house (Acts 10). It was there that he saw the Gentiles filled with the Holy Spirit just as the Jewish believers were filled at Pentecost.

GREATER THAN A GOLD MINE

"Whereof I was made a minister, according to the gift of the grace of God given unto me by the effectual working of his power. Unto me, who am less than the least of all saints, is this grace given, that I should preach among the Gentiles the unsearchable riches of Christ" (Ephesians 3:7, 8).

"Unsearchable riches"! That was the way Paul felt about the gospel. The worldly man cannot comprehend this. If he found a gold mine he would call

51

that "riches." But to call something you can't see with your physical eyes "riches" is unthinkable to the carnal mind.

The only way to search out these riches is by the help of the Holy Spirit. He knows right where you are. He also knows how much of the truth you are able to receive at a time.

Riches is an attractive word. The human heart is stirred at the thought of it. Men have sacrificed everything with the hope of becoming rich. Unfortunately, earthly riches are disappointing. Their glitter fades. They can be stolen or destroyed. The happiness they promise often does not materialize. In fact, wealth may even cause grief and heartache. And we cannot take it with us when we die.

Not so with the unsearchable riches of Christ. Their value grows with every passing day. We appreciate them more and more as we search them out. There are no disappointments in Christ's riches. They cannot be stolen or destroyed. They are eternal. Death cannot tear them from our grasp.

Paul had been a fierce persecutor of the church. He could not get over the fact that such a person could be rescued by the grace of God. Imagine a Christ-hater like Saul of Tarsus becoming one of the greatest champions of the gospel! Paul did not hesitate to refer to himself as the chiefest of sinners. He knew he was a spiritual pauper apart from Christ. This made him appreciate those spiritual riches all the more.

What do we have that we did not receive from God? If we are rich in grace it is because Christ has made us that way.

If we possess Christ we have the Source of all

riches. Everything we need we find in Him. We do not receive all of our riches in one day. The Lord scatters His jewels along our path through a whole lifetime. This is what makes being a Christian so thrilling.

GOD IS SO WISE

"And to make all men see what is the fellowship of the mystery, which from the beginning of the world hath been hid in God, who created all things by Jesus Christ: to the intent that now unto the principalities and powers in heavenly places might be known by the church the manifold wisdom of God" (Ephesians 3:9, 10).

Manifold means "many-fold." The wisdom of God is made up of many folds. We unfold one part of the gospel and revel in it. Then we unfold another and another, and still we have not reached the end. We are always discovering something new in Christ.

The fact that God, in His wisdom, sometimes hides things from us does not mean that He is unkind. It suits His plan and purpose to make known some things at certain times. Jesus told His disciples before His crucifixion that He had many things to say to them for which they were not yet ready.

The time was not ripe for the revelation of the mystery of the Church until Jesus died and rose again. In our individual lives there are things God cannot reveal to us until an appropriate time. Jesus told Peter, "What I do thou knowest not now; but thou shalt know hereafter" (John 13:7). It was impossible for Peter to understand the things Jesus was telling him until after His resurrection.

After the outpouring of the Spirit at Pentecost all of the disciples understood truths that had been mysteries to them before. The Holy Spirit is the great Teacher of the Church. He is the Interpreter of the Word.

Our understanding will be imperfect as long as we are in this world. But as we walk with the Lord we will continually see more truths unfold.

The "principalities and powers in heavenly places" are probably fallen angels. Even these beings have seen, in a measure, the coming triumph of Christ's kingdom. Every time a soul is saved it demonstrates to Satan and his hosts that they are doomed.

Man considers himself wise, but how far behind God he is. The smallest thought that enters God's mind is greater than man's biggest. We bow in humility before "the manifold wisdom of God." How wonderful that He chooses to share a measure of it with His children.

There is a responsibility on our part to *seek* truth. Undoubtedly there are many things still hidden from us only because we do not take the time to search for them. A lazy-minded Christian is not going to acquire much spiritual knowledge.

The Divine Purpose

"According to the eternal purpose which he purposed in Christ Jesus our Lord" (Ephesians 3:11).

The Church is not an afterthought of God. It is part of His eternal plan. Men may flounder along, improvising schemes as they go, but not God. His purposes are established long before He acts.

God's purpose in establishing the Church existed from eternity past. The Lord Jesus Christ was the only One who could execute that purpose. The mightiest angel could not do it. Jesus had to carry out redemption's plan. This, of course, made it possible for the Church to be born.

Not only does God have an overall purpose that encompasses the universe, He also has one for each individual life. "All things work together for good to them that love God, to them who are the called according to his purpose" (Romans 8:28). The Christian's life is not a series of accidents. He does not have to depend on luck. He need not carry a rabbit's foot or four-leaf clover. Nor is it necessary for him to have his horoscope read. The believer's life is not influenced by the stars or planets. God's plan has no relation to the zodiac.

The Christian is tied into a plan older than the universe. That plan was in the mind of God long before He created the world. We are told in 2 Timothy 1:9: "Who hath saved us, and called us with a holy calling, not according to our works, but according to his own purpose and grace, which was given us in Christ Jesus before the world began."

God had a purpose in choosing Abraham and his descendants. They were to show His glory and His laws to the world. They were to prepare mankind for the coming of the Messiah. The purpose of the Church is likewise to testify to the world concerning God and His plan of redemption. The Lord has no other way of conveying His message of salvation to a lost world except through the Church.

If a carpenter doesn't start building a house without a blueprint, surely the Lord has a blueprint for each life. If we are wise we will try to discover God's plan for us. We should endeavor to fit in where He wants us. It is not our business to please ourselves, but to please Him.

Nothing that God's enemies do will defeat His

purpose. They are trying hard, but they are doomed to defeat. Communism will not destroy the Church. Satan has always tried to outwit God, but his failures are a matter of record.

BOLDNESS AND CONFIDENCE

"In whom we have boldness and access with confidence by the faith of him" (Ephesians 3:12).

When we speak of our boldness in God we are not talking about the irreverent kind of boldness. It is simply a feeling of ease in His presence. We enjoy being close to Him. Our happiest moments are spent communing with Him.

Those who lived under the Law were not bold. When God gave the Law on Mount Sinai everyone was terrified. Even Moses was stricken with fear.

But now we are in the Church Age. This is the dispensation of grace. God has extended an invitation to everyone to come to Him. This is made possible, of course, only because Jesus' blood has been shed.

There is a boldness that is rude and presumptuous. Familiarity breeds contempt, and we must not try to use that kind of familiarity with God. Christians are bold because they know Jesus has finished the work of redemption for them. They know that they are God's children, and that a home is being prepared in heaven for them. Their boldness is a quiet sense of security that comes through faith.

If we tried to come into God's presence with our sins still clinging to us we would be terrified. We could not stand it. But our sins have been washed away. We come with a clean record. God's ears are open to our cry. His eye never ceases to look upon us. This makes us bold.

It was not *our* faith that made the way of access to God, it was Christ's: "The faith of him." Through faith we are united with the Lord Jesus, and what is His is ours. Christ's faith gave Him victory over Satan. It gave Him strength to face the Cross. Through his faithfulness we triumph over Satan and walk the overcomers' path.

As members of the true Church we stand in a new relationship to God. This makes our access to Him continuous. It is free and unrestricted. Our confidence is not in ourselves, but in Christ. He is our High Priest and Mediator.

God is bigger than anything we may face. When we commit our cause to Him we too are bigger than our problems. This is the way to victorious living.

The day of human priests and sacrifices is past. The veil has been rent. The way into the Holy of Holies is open. God's hands are extended. He says, "Come." The blood of Jesus has destroyed the obstacles that stood between us and the Heavenly Father. In Christ we are now a part of the heavenly family.

Do You Belong to the Church?

Church membership is important. Every Christian should be a member of a Christ-honoring church. The Bible commands us not to forsake the assembling of ourselves together. Anyone who says he can worship God anywhere and doesn't have to go to church is simply "copping out."

It does not build Christian character to float from one church to another. Church-hopping is often practiced by those who wish to glean all the blessings without taking any responsibility. Each of us needs a stable Christian fellowship, a pastor, and a church home. We should not only be attenders, but members. We should give the church our complete support—spiritually, financially, and by our regular presence.

Unfortunately, some have made church membership synonymous with salvation. To the question, "Are you a Christian?" they will reply, "Yes, I have belonged to the church for many years." To be an unsaved church member is a tragedy, but it is repeated often.

The church of which Paul writes is the *true* Church. It is made up of all born-again believers. Its members are those washed in Jesus' blood. Their sins are forgiven. Their names are written in the Lamb's Book of Life as well as on the church roster.

It is regrettable that the Church is split into so many denominations, but this need not keep anyone from living a useful Christian life. After one is saved he belongs to the true Church, and he should set out to find a local church that will provide him with spiritual nourishment.

Nothing we can do in our own strength can make us members of Christ's true church. Water baptism, taking communion, saying prayers, reciting ritual—all of these are in vain if we are depending on them for our salvation. There is only one way into the true Church, and that is the way of the Cross. The road we must travel is called "repentance." This means a complete turning from sin.

When we finally stand before God He will not ask us what local church we belonged to. He will be concerned with one thing only: "Did you accept my Son as your Lord and personal Saviour during your days of life?" This is something that has to be settled while we are still alive and conscious.

7
Strength and Power

"That he would grant you, according to the riches of his glory, to be strengthened with might by his Spirit" (Ephesians 3:16).

Here is a glimpse into the apostle's heart. He says, "I'm praying for you." Then he tells a few of the things he is praying for.

Above all, Paul wanted these Christians to be strong. That strength must come from one Source— the Holy Spirit. We are victorious to the extent the Spirit possesses us. We can't do things that grieve Him and expect to be overcomers. We must keep up our prayer life and Bible study. We must maintain our separation from the world.God's house must occupy a central place in our weekly schedule. Christian fellowship is essential. All of these things help keep us in the place where the Spirit can possess us and bless us.

"Not by might, nor by power, but by my Spirit, saith the Lord"(Zechariah 4:6). That's an Old Testament promise, but it's just as true today. There is no salvation apart from the Spirit. There is no daily victory over temptation without His strength. Jesus was anointed by the Spirit before He faced Satan in the wilderness. It was by the Spirit's power and the use of the Word that our Saviour drove the enemy off the battlefield in defeat.

"Strengthened with might" suggests strength piled upon strength. There is no limit to the strength the Spirit gives. It is limited only by our faith. It is given "according to the riches of his glory," and you can't ask for more than that!

Paul experienced the baptism in the Holy Spirit after his conversion. He saw many filled with the Spirit during his ministry. He constantly emphasized the necessity of staying full of the Spirit (Ephesians 5:18).

Jesus promised in Acts 1:8 that the Spirit's coming upon believers would be with power. We have no power apart from the Spirit's indwelling. This power is not only for witnessing, but for overcoming. It is the only power that Satan fears.

The Holy Spirit is the Comforter Jesus promised before He went away. Much of His conversation with His disciples before the Cross centered on this great truth (John 14-16). Jesus returned to His Father's right hand, but He did not leave us comfortless. He has sent the Spirit to empower us and lead us into great victories in our daily living. May we walk in the Spirit and be led by the Spirit—always.

TAKE CARE OF THAT INNER MAN!

"Strengthened . . . in the inner man" (Ephesians 3:16).

Actions start on the inside. We are controlled by our hearts. The outward man is important, but the inward man is too. When sin shows itself outwardly it is because it has developed inwardly. "As he thinketh in his heart, so is he" (Proverbs 23:7).

Jesus laid strong emphasis on the inner life. In

Matthew 15:18-20 He said: "But those things which proceed out of the mouth come forth from the heart; and they defile the man. For out of the heart proceed evil thoughts, murders, adulteries, fornications, thefts, false witness, blasphemies: these are the things which defile a man: but to eat with unwashen hands defileth not a man."

Are we as careful to keep our hearts clean as we are to keep our bodies clean? The condition of the inner man determines the condition of the outer man. Never forget it!

The Bible teaches us not only to be clean inwardly, but also to be strong. The "inner man" to which Paul refers is, of course, the whole inner life—the emotions, feelings, motives, and character.

Our bodies can't be kept strong unless they are fed. Neither can the inner man. He must be fed on the Bible. He must be sustained by prayer and worship. It is sad to see someone who pampers his body but neglects his soul. The person who does this will not survive the devil's attacks. He will be an easy prey to temptation. He just won't be able to take life's blows and maintain his Christian faith.

We don't know how much strength we have until it is tested. Many seem to be well grounded until a test comes. Then their lack of inner power causes them to fall.

Man does not live by bread alone. He has spiritual needs that can only be met by feeding his spirit on the Word of God. Our outward man is perishing day by day the Bible says. We are getting closer to the grave all the time. Someday that outward man will be struck down by death. But the *real* man—the inner, spiritual part of us—will live on forever.

Our inner life is weakened by reading filthy literature, watching questionable scenes on TV, listening to unwholesome music all day long, and many other things indulged in by so many. We must be on guard against anything that will erode that inner strength we need so much.

CHRIST IN YOUR HEART

"That Christ may dwell in your hearts by faith; that ye, being rooted and grounded in love, may be able to comprehend with all saints what is the breadth, and length, and depth, and height" (Ephesians 3:17, 18).

It is not enough to have casual visits from Christ. He must indwell our hearts always. He must make His home there continually.

The indwelling Christ beautifies life at its source. He sanctifies the thoughts, motives, and ambitions before they can become actions. He deals with the will.

It is beyond the mental capacity of the natural man to comprehend the things of God. Spiritual truths can be grasped only by spiritual minds and hearts. The Ephesians, like all other Christians, could not begin to understand God's program for this age. They needed to be enlightened by the Holy Spirit. Without such enlightenment a believer will remain carnal and shallow. The grace of God has dimensions beyond the grasp of natural understanding.

Christ must never be given second place. He must always be at the center of our lives. As Christians we must be Christ-possessed. To use everyday language, Christ must be in the driver's seat, not simply riding as a passenger.

The effect of Christ's indwelling is to root and

ground the heart in love. Such love will shine out in our relationships with others.

Before He left this world, Jesus promised His disciples to be personally present with them always. This is a promise He has kept. His presence touches our thoughts and affections. It inspires in our hearts a love of the truth and a desire to do God's will. This presence is enjoyed by faith. It is wonderfully real to the true believer.

It is not merely the doctrine of Christ, His example, or the memory of Him that dwells in the believing heart—it is His very presence. The Christian is united with Christ by the Holy Spirit.

There is much in our nature, even after salvation, that is not pleasing to the Lord. Christ comes in to remedy these faults. As He lives within He mellows us, sweetens us, changes our disposition, sanctifies our interests, and draws us farther and farther away from the influence of this ungodly age.

BEYOND KNOWLEDGE

"And to know the love of Christ, which passeth knowledge" (Ephesians 3:19).

Again we have a subject too great for the natural intellect. The love of Christ surpasses knowledge. It can be understood only as He reveals it to us. The more we are filled with His fullness, the more we understand His love.

Many have rejected the gospel because it is beyond their human comprehension. There are many ways in which the truth does not coincide with their thinking. This is an "age of reason." Many are still unwilling to accept what they cannot understand or explain.

There are many things in the natural realm that are beyond our understanding; yet we accept them. It is inconsistent to ignore Christ's love because it cannot be understood.

Who could possibly comprehend what took place in the heart of God when He "so loved the world"? Who can understand what it meant for Him to give His only begotten Son to die for men's sins? Who can fathom the compassion for sinners which kept Jesus on the cross when He might have come down and saved himself? The love of God is the greatest challenge to the human intellect in the whole universe. It is so far beyond the intellect that the only way to explain it is in Paul's words: It "passeth knowledge."

The believer who becomes deeply rooted in Christ's love will not easily fall prey to the devil's schemes. The more he thinks of God's love for him the more he will, in turn, love God.

The one filled with Christ's love will have an attractive Christian life. He will draw others to the Lord. He will be an encouragement to fellow believers.

The love of Christ gives strength in weakness. It gives patience during trials. It imparts grace in everyday living and hope in dying. It brings heaven closer to earth.

The love of Christ is not a passing shadow. It is not a bubble that will soon burst. It is not based on our feelings but on the very character of God. When that great, overpowering love becomes the controlling factor in our lives the world will truly see Jesus in us. And Satan will certainly have a hard time gaining an entrance into our hearts.

There is a difference in knowing *about* something and having a personal experience with it. It is not enough to know *about* Christ's love. We must know it personally. It must become a daily experience in our lives.

EXCEEDING ABUNDANTLY ABOVE

"That ye might be filled with all the fullness of God. Now unto him that is able to do exceeding abundantly above all that we ask or think, according to the power that worketh in us, unto him be glory in the church by Christ Jesus throughout all ages, world without end. Amen" (Ephesians 3:19-21).

This is a doxology. Paul is launching into a rapturous burst of praise. He cannot contain himself as he writes of the love of Christ. He must give vent to his pent-up feelings of adoration for the Saviour. Note that it is all addressed "unto him."

The Christian should always be full of God. The miracle is that God would condescend to fill a human life with himself.

The converted heart has the capacity to receive the things of God. Of course, we never receive *all* of God. He is too great for that. We should be constantly praying, "Lord, enlarge me so I may contain more of Thee."

When we are full of God there is no room for anything else. Sanctification is simply getting so full of the Lord that there is no room for sin. Rules and regulations can never drive the world out of a man's heart. But when he becomes full of God, things of the world will automatically be pushed out.

As we are filled with God there is less room for doubt and fear. The most peaceful soul in the world is the one full of God. There is no room in his heart for disturbing thoughts. "Perfect love casteth out fear" (1 John 4:18).

Paul employs strong language to tell us what God is able to do for us. "Exceeding abundantly above," he says. What God can do for us is so far above what we can even imagine that words fail us.

What God does for us depends on the extent to which we accept His power in our lives. It is "according to the power that *worketh* in us." There is never a shortage of God's power, but our lack of faith can keep it from *working* in us. This causes us to live below our Christian privileges. Let's not limit God by our unbelief!

For a Christian to live a defeated life is like someone starving to death in the midst of plenty. It is like dying of thirst while living beside a lake. God's grace is like a great ocean that cannot possibly be exhausted. If we live below our privileges we have only ourselves to blame.

STAYING ON TOP

It is not enough merely to be a believer. God's will is that we also be overcomers. The world is not to stay on top of us. We are to stay on top of it!

It is completely inconsistent for anyone to live the Christian life carelessly or haphazardly. Anything worth doing at all is worth doing well. This is especially true in the spiritual realm.

A defeated Christian is a poor advertisement for the gospel. A victorious one is the best advertisement possible.

Defeat is a state of mind. If we think defeat we will experience it. Victory starts in our thinking. We must keep our thoughts centered on the victory Christ bought for us on the cross. We have to keep our eyes off circumstances, people, and things.

We can spend so much time looking at our own

shortcomings and faults that we will be discouraged. "Looking unto Jesus" must be the watchword of the Christian life.

Christianity is more than a creed. It is a Person. It is more than embracing certain doctrines. It is a matter of having Christ in our life in all of His fullness. This brings victory. This makes overcomers of us. We cannot defeat our enemies in our own strength, but Christ can.

God's resources are ours in Christ. The power of the Holy Spirit is ours. The Word of God is our weapon. We are more than conquerors through Him who loved us.

Of course we are in a battle. This age is hostile to Christian living. But that should be a challenge to the Christian, not a reason for giving up. The greater the battle, the sweeter the victory.

Satan is a defeated enemy. Jesus struck him the deathblow on the cross. He sealed His victory by His resurrection and ascension. This is the ground for all our hopes. We rest in the finished work of Christ. What He accomplished for us is indeed "exceeding abundantly above" our powers of comprehension. But Christ's victory was real, and our victory in Him is real. There is nothing imaginary about the overcoming life. It is within the reach of every Blood-washed child of God.

8

The "Other Comforter" at Work

Jesus came to establish a Church. Pentecost was that Church's birthday. Until the Holy Spirit was poured out the Church could not have existed. The Spirit is the Church's life. He is the Overseer, the Superintendent, the Shepherd of the Church. Christ is gone from earth physically, and He has given the care of His church into the hands of the One He promised to send after He went back to heaven.

A church that does not have the Spirit's presence is nothing but a religious shell. It has no real life. It can never accomplish the work of God.

A church is made up of people—you and you and you. Just as a wall is built of individual bricks, the church is built of individual souls. If one brick is missing it is noticeable. There is a place for everyone. So it is in the church.

The pulpit is not the only place of service in the church. If we are open to the Spirit's leading He will guide each one of us into just the place of service where He knows we will fit. If we cannot find our place in the church it is because we are not completely yielded to the Spirit—or we do not *understand* His leading.

Never should we worry over someone else's ministry in the Church. If it seems to attract more attention than our work this is no cause for envy or jealousy. The Head of the Church knows where the talents and abilities of each individual will fit. He does not place square pegs in round holes. He puts us where we can accomplish the most for His glory.

Each Christian has a relationship to the Holy Spirit and a relationship to other believers. The Church is not a disorganized mob. It is a Body. It is God's will that the Body function efficiently. This is why the Spirit is constantly at work in the Church. How patient He is! We learn our lessons slowly, but He keeps trying to help us. He is a Master Teacher and wants to lead us from one level of spiritual understanding to another. In this way our service to Christ and the Church will be enhanced.

This is His church; not ours. We are to let our lights shine before men so they may glorify the Lord. He uses men in the building of His kingdom. He must have human hearts, hands, and feet to accomplish His mission. God grant that ours may always be yielded to Him.

True Oneness

"Endeavoring to keep the unity of the Spirit in the bond of peace. There is one body, and one Spirit, even as ye are called in one hope of your calling" (Ephesians 4:3, 4).

Jesus' prayer for His church is that they may be one. Such unity is not easily achieved. God must work with humans, and human nature is not always pliable—even to His hands. It takes some "endeavoring" on the part of all of us to preserve the unity Christ desires.

Every believer must watch carefully for any signs of discord and guard against them. They should be nipped in the bud. They must not be allowed to spread.

Paul is not talking about the kind of unity man can produce by his own efforts. He is not discussing the kind of outward unity sought by champions of the ecumenical movement. You can merge every denomination into one and still not have real unity. The unity of which Paul speaks is "of the Spirit." The Spirit is the Author of it.

There were factions in the churches of Paul's day. He waged relentless war against them. He rebuked Christians for allowing such things. The Church is surrounded by enemies. It cannot afford to be torn apart by internal strife. God's people must present a united front.

The greatest enemy of the unity of the Spirit is the natural selfishness and pride of men. Everyone has a tendency to push his own ideas. Many contend fiercely for goals they have set.

The members of the Church must be considerate of one another. They must avoid undue criticism and condemnation. They must be merciful and forgiving. Above all, they must maintain a walk in the Spirit that will prevent them from giving in to the impulses of the flesh.

The Church has a heavenly calling, but it must pay close attention to its earthly conduct. Men may not be reading their Bibles, but they are reading us!

One of the scriptural symbols of the Holy Spirit is the dove. A dove is a gentle bird that is easily frightened. Disunity and discord drive away the Holy Spirit quickly. He can dwell only in an atmosphere of peace. And we are responsible for maintaining such an atmosphere.

Christians are not in competition with each other.

They are fellow laborers striving for the same cause. They are responsible to the same Master.

CHRIST'S GIFTS TO HIS CHURCH

"But unto every one of us is given grace according to the measure of the gift of Christ. Wherefore he saith, when he ascended up on high, he led captivity captive, and gave gifts unto men" (Ephesians 4:7, 8).

Not every member of the Church has the same gift. Christ measures out His gifts. Each one receives "according to the measure." The "grace" referred to here reminds us that we have no room for boasting about what we have received from God.

Verse 8 refers to Psalm 68:18. It pictures Christ's victory and ascension, by which He triumphed over all evil and became the Head of the Church. When the commander of an ancient army defeated the enemy he took spoils and made prisoners of the opposing army. Paul uses this kind of terminology to describe Christ's victory over His enemies.

No Christian should ever say, "The church doesn't need me." Neither should he think, "There is no place for me in the church." According to Paul, "Every one of us" receives God's grace through the Holy Spirit's ministry. This grace is for the individual's spiritual growth. It is also for the strengthening of the whole Church.

We should use our spiritual gifts unselfishly and in the fear of God. Since everyone receives a different gift and all gifts are needed in the Church, we are mutually dependent on one another. Each one should exercise his ministry faithfully, otherwise the Church will suffer.

The grace of which Paul speaks is not given in equal measure to all. It is not our place to question why one Christian receives a ministry that is more conspicuous than another. This is a matter entirely in the hands of the Lord.

God has wisely assembled our physical body. He knew where each part belonged and what it would contribute to the whole. He is also wise in the way He has assembled Christ's body, the Church. He knows where each one of us will do the most good, and He puts us in that place.

The true unity of the Church is promoted when each one performs his function for the good of the whole. Our chief concern must be for the Body; not for ourselves. It is a privilege to serve the Lord, no matter how humble that service may seem.

Let no believer complain, "I have no gift." Paul declares that "every one of us" is included in God's distribution. We must not try to avoid our responsibilities by claiming a lack of ability

GIFTED MEN

"And he gave some, apostles; and some, prophets; and some, evangelists; and some, pastors and teachers; for the perfecting of the saints, for the work of the ministry, for the edifying of the body of Christ: till we all come in the unity of the faith, and of the knowledge of the Son of God, unto a perfect man, unto the measure of the stature of the fullness of Christ" (Ephesians 4:11-13).

Paul speaks here of the gifted men who are in positions of leadership in the Church. The organization of the Church is not a human arrangement. It is ordained of God. Its leaders are divinely appointed. Paul declared that gifted men are themselves God's gifts to the Church.

The full catalog of gifts is not given in detail in this

passage. Not every Christian is an apostle, prophet, evangelist, pastor, or teacher. But all Spirit-filled Christians do have a ministry.

First Corinthians 12:8-10 lists nine gifts which should be in operation in the Church: the word of wisdom, the word of knowledge, faith, the gifts of healing, the working of miracles, prophecy, discerning of spirits, tongues, and interpretation of tongues. These are not limited to those in positions of leadership. The Spirit divides them to "every man severally as he will" (1 Corinthians 12:11).

It is true that these gifts have often been abused. As long as the Church is on earth they will continue to be abused at times. But this must not cause us to shun the gifts. It is Satan's business to cause people to become misguided. Under his prodding they place too much emphasis on some aspects of the supernatural. Some may react by deciding the gifts should be completely eliminated. This must not be allowed to happen. We should humbly ask God's guidance in maintaining balance in these matters.

If we would confine ourselves to the Bible we would not go astray in our interpretation of spiritual gifts. There is ample teaching in the Word to give us an understanding in these matters.

In addition to the gifts already mentioned, Paul sets forth three more ministries in 1 Corinthians 12:28: teaching, helps, and governments. Thank God for our teachers, our administrators, and those able to help anywhere they are needed in God's work.

No gift can be properly exercised apart from the continuous anointing of the Spirit. Neither can it be effective unless it is used in love.

"That we henceforth be no more children, tossed to and fro, and carried about with every wind of doctrine, by the sleight of men, and cunning craftiness, whereby they lie in wait to deceive" (Ephesians 4:14).

Our spiritual experience is very much like our natural life. We enter the world as babies. We pass through childhood and eventually reach maturity. Our thinking as adults is certainly different than when we were children. Experience gives us a wider perspective and broadens our outlook.

Spiritually we are babes in Christ at first. It takes time to get settled in our Christian experience. We do not know all of the doctrines of the Bible at first. We have not experienced trials and temptations. But in a normal Christian life one advances beyond the childhood state and becomes a strong, stable Christian who is capable of teaching and helping others.

One mark of childhood is fickleness. Children are changeable. They are unsettled in their thinking. One of the ministries of the Spirit is to change that. He endeavors to produce spiritual stability and maturity in us. Helping each Christian from babyhood to adulthood is no small task. How fortunate that we have the Spirit to accomplish this work in us. How patiently He leads us from the ABC's of the gospel to deeper truths. He shields the young Christian from trials that would prove too hard for him. Later on he permits the tests to become more difficult so spiritual strength may be developed.

In our experience with the Lord we often have a great deal of feeling and emotion at first. The Spirit permits this. But as time goes on the child of God must learn to walk by faith rather than sight. For this reason there are seasons when the Lord may withhold feeling. This is to teach us to rely on the Bible rather than on changeable human impulses.

The Spirit uses the Word of God as the chief instrument in bringing the Christian to maturity. The one who leaves his Bible on the shelf is depriving himself of the Spirit's food for his soul. His growth will be stunted and he will lack the strength he needs to fight the good fight of faith. There will be little depth to his experience.

"No more children." This is God's will for us. It pleases an earthly parent to see physical growth in his child. Certainly it gladdens the heart of our Heavenly Father to see spiritual growth in His children. Let's grow up!

"THE HEAD, EVEN CHRIST"

"But speaking the truth in love, may grow up into him in all things, which is the head, even Christ: from whom the whole body fitly joined together and compacted by that which every joint supplieth, according to the effectual working in the measure of every part, maketh increase of the body unto the edifying of itself in love" (Ephesians 4:15, 16).

Other religions involve intellectual assent to a creed. Christianity involves a vital union between the believer and a living Person, the Lord Jesus.

Jesus had this in mind when He prayed concerning himself and His disciples in John 17:23, "I in them." He also illustrated this union in John 15 when He compared himself to a vine and Christians to the branches.

Our union with Christ also unites us with one another. Physically speaking the head directs the actions of the body through the brain. By their relationship to the head, the members of the body bear a relationship to one another. By their response to the impulses of the brain, the hands, feet, eyes, and ears work in harmony. When a Christian is truly united to Christ he will feel a deep sense of unity and harmony with other Christians.

Love plays a great part in all of this. We should not only speak the truth, but speak it "in love," Paul declares. Verse 16 says that the Church edifies itself in love. There is no way to separate love from Christian growth.

Union with Christ produces natural and normal growth. It is unhealthy for one part of the Body to grow abnormally. Each member should develop to its proper size. It must not be out of proportion to the rest of the Body. We Pentecostals face the danger of overstressing spiritual manifestations without emphasizing equally the fruit of the Spirit and the development of Christian character. Staying close to Christ helps us keep everything in proper perspective.

The Church should never come to the place where it stops growing. If it does it is out of fellowship with its living Lord. The goal toward which we move is that of perfect comformity to Christ. The more we grow spiritually the more we will be like Him.

9
The New Man

Salvation is a new life. The Christian turns his back on sin. His example is Christ. He strives to be like Him in all things.

To be like Christ is to be *holy*. This is a word that should not frighten us. A truly holy life is attractive and beautiful. Genuine holiness calls attention to Christ rather than self. A holy person is the best advertisement the gospel has.

In the spring of the year new life is evident everywhere. The trees begin putting on new leaves. Buds appear. Flowers start to blossom. All of this is the result of new life surging through the world of nature. It is a time of great beauty.

The holy life is simply a case of the new life of Christ showing itself in the believer. Man cannot produce leaves and flowers. Neither can he produce true holiness. Christ's life in us is what makes the fruit of holiness appear.

Jesus said we are known by our fruit. If someone professes salvation but does not exhibit holiness there is reason to doubt that his experience is genuine.

There is both a positive and negative side to holiness. The Christian must say "Yes" to God and "No" to sin. There are things he does, and things he does not do.

The Christians to whom Paul wrote his letters were just a step away from their old pagan lives. The churches then were like islands in a sea of heathenism. Believers lived in an atmosphere teeming with sin and corruption. It was necessary for Paul to warn them against letting the old things creep back into their lives.

We, too, live in a world whose atmosphere is poisoned with sin. To be holy requires constant vigilance. Our guard can never be let down. The devil must be resisted. Holiness must be "followed . . . after" (Hebrews 12:14).

According to Jesus' teaching, Christians are the salt of the earth. They are the light of the world. This means that they cannot isolate themselves. They cannot seal themselves off from society. They are to be in the world, yet not a part of the world. Is it possible to live this way? By the grace and power of God, yes. If holiness were an impossible goal the Lord would never have pointed us to it. He does not taunt us by issuing challenges He knows we can never meet. He loves us too much for that.

NEW CLOTHES

"That ye put off concerning the former conversation the old man, which is corrupt according to the deceitful lusts; and be renewed in the spirit of your mind; and that ye put on the new man, which after God is created in righteousness and true holiness" (Ephesians 4:22-24).

Paul implies that the sinner is like a man wearing filthy, tattered rags. When Christ comes into the heart there is a change. The "old man" with his rags

78

is cast off. A completely new man is put on. The old man and his clothes are not patched or mended; they are completely discarded.

Paul is not complimentary of the "old man." He says he is corrupt, deceitful, and lustful. He is utterly unfit for heaven and the presence of God. He cannot be reformed or made more attractive. He is of the devil. Morally and spiritually he is steadily deteriorating.

The renewal Paul speaks of is the work of the Holy Spirit. Christians are to long for such a renewal. They are to pray for it and strive for it.

The principles and attitudes of the "new man" are in line with the character and person of Christ. It is like a change of clothes. Instead of the old rags, the Christian wears beautiful new garments. Those garments are called "holiness."

The lusts of the old nature are deceitful because they promise what they cannot deliver. Instead of happiness and liberty they bring sorrow and pain. What are lusts? They are legitimate desires carried to the extreme; thus, they become sin. From the very beginning sin has distorted and twisted things that are proper and right.

This renewal must be on the inside of us. Salvation deals with the inner life first. Of course, the outward life is eventually affected. But to start on the outside is merely to deal with symptoms while ignoring the disease.

The heart of man is deceitful and corrupt, so it is the heart with which the Holy Spirit must deal. Paul says the Christian has "the mind of Christ" (1 Corinthians 2:16). Christ's mind was free from hatred, lust, jealousy, and envy, and ours must be too if we are to be His true followers.

Under the Old Testament the laws of God were written on tables of stone. Man looked at them and tried to obey them, but failed. Under the New Testament the Holy Spirit writes those laws in our heart. We obey them because we love God and want to please Him.

In God's Image

In scriptural language *heart* and *mind* are closely connected. The mind, of course, is the seat of the intellect, while the heart is the seat of love, affection, and emotion. Both the mind and heart must be changed. Our thoughts have to be renewed. So do our affections. Salvation is a thorough work. Holiness must invade every part of our beings.

The new man is created "after God," Paul says. This means he is created in God's image. The first man, Adam, was brought into being by a creative act of God. The "new man" Paul talks about is also a creation of the Lord. Note that he is "created . . . in true holiness." There is a false holiness that is only outward. It was the sort the Pharisees flaunted. Many today have only a form of righteousness. But true holiness occurs when the new man is created in the very righteousness of the Lord himself. It is the only kind of righteousness God can accept.

What kind of righteousness characterizes the new man? Integrity, honesty, fair and open dealings, and good deeds in everyday life. There is deep reverence for God and for truth. The righteous person will be in sympathy with God's will in all things. Christianity demands a life of high standards and practice.

Holy living is not something a Christian can indulge in only while in church. It must show itself daily. If it doesn't, there is reason to wonder what kind of holiness it is.

We are living epistles, "known and read of all men" (2 Corinthians 3:2). The world can see our faith only as it sees our works. James is very careful to teach this throughout his epistle. Our lights must shine before men continually. Why? So they may see our good works and glorify our Father in heaven (Matthew 5:16).

"Righteousness and true holiness." This is God's goal for everyone who professes to be His child. We cannot hide behind the failures of others. Neither can we excuse ourselves because of our environment. Holiness is a "must."

It was no accident that Jesus called salvation a new birth. A birth is the beginning of a brand-new life. There is something so fresh and pure about a baby. It is not an old life that has been patched up or remodeled. It is new. So it is with salvation.

If the world has a low view of Christian living, some of the blame must be laid at the door of Christians. It's easy to forget that God has no representatives in this world but us.

Don't Give Satan an Opening!

"Wherefore putting away lying, speak every man truth with his neighbor: for we are members one of another. Be ye angry, and sin not: let not the sun go down upon your wrath: neither give place to the devil. Let him that stole steal no more: but rather let him labor, working with his hands the thing which is good, that he may have to give to him that needeth" (Ephesians 4:25-28).

The battle isn't over when we are saved. It has just started. For this reason the Christian life is one of continual resistance. No opening must be given to Satan—not even a small one. He must be shut out. It is dangerous to give him even an inch. He will soon take a mile, then another mile, and another.

Paul speaks of "putting away" sins. This involves effort on our part. One of the things we are to put away, he declares, is lying. Falsehood is a common human vice. It is a mark of fallen humanity. In fact, lying is one of the earliest manifestations of sin in one's life.

How often are we tempted to practice deceit. We may not lie outright, but we may use subterfuge in small ways. We may leave false impressions. A silent lie is as bad as any other.

And there is anger. It would seem that Paul is not completely forbidding anger, but cautions Christians to beware of letting it cause them to sin. Bitterness and spite are by-products of anger; so is hatred. Anger can even lead to murder. It must never be allowed to get out of hand in a Christian's life.

The literal translation of verse 28 is: "Let the stealer steal no more." The Christian is a giver, a sharer—not a stealer. What he has he acquires by hard work. He will not take advantage of his fellowman in any way. It may seem strange to warn Christians about stealing, but we must remember there is more than one way to steal. What about cheating on your income tax return? Falsifying any type of record for the purpose of gain is certainly theft. The Christian life is one of unbroken honesty toward God and man.

Any one of these sins can make an opening for Satan. He doesn't need a big one. He is an expert at slipping in through small cracks!

This business of resisting the devil requires endless self-discipline. It takes fierce determination. It takes prayer. The Word of God is our greatest weapon in the battle. We must not absent ourselves from church services. Each of us is strengthened by the other. We're in the fight together.

WATCH YOUR TONGUE!

"Let no corrupt communication proceed out of your mouth, but that which is good to the use of edifying, that it may minister grace unto the hearers. And grieve not the Holy Spirit of God, whereby ye are sealed unto the day of redemption. Let all bitterness, and wrath, and anger, and clamor, and evil speaking, be put away from you, with all malice" (Ephesians 4:29-31).

Sins of speech are among the most common. The Christian's lips should give forth only what is wholesome and pure. Is it even necessary to say that profanity and vulgarity must have no place in Christian conversation? The believer must also avoid the empty and frivolous talk that is characteristic of people who don't know Christ.

There is a lot of meaning in that expression "corrupt communication." It includes all manner of speech that is not sound and wholesome. When a Christian talks he is not merely to make conversation. His purpose is to help, to bless, and to uplift those who are listening to him.

Obscene jokes, foolish jesting, silly songs, and unclean suggestions are completely inconsistent with the Christian life. They are to be shunned at all times. Christian lips should be sanctified. They should speak only what is pleasing to God.

Certainly gossip is included in the category of "corrupt communication." The Christian does not seek to hurt the character or reputation of anyone. He does not enjoy conversation that maligns others. The old adage "Think twice before you speak once" is still good today.

We are temples of the Holy Spirit. Paul indicates that "corrupt communication" grieves the Holy Spirit. Anything that would cause Him to withdraw His influence and grace from our lives should be avoided completely. Our Christian life depends on the Spirit's continued ministry to us. By Him we are sealed until the day of redemption.

Verse 31 deals with the general temper and disposition of the Christian. Notice the chain reaction: bitterness leads to wrath, which leads to all of the other sins mentioned. The whole thing is to be stopped before it even gets started.

Speech and temper go together. What comes out of the mouth starts on the inside. Stern discipline must be exercised over our thoughts, motives, and attitudes. These govern our conversation. If we take care of our hearts, our lips will take care of themselves.

LEND A HELPING HAND

"And be ye kind one to another, tender-hearted, forgiving one another, even as God for Christ's sake hath forgiven you" (Ephesians 4:32).

These characteristics are the exact opposites of those named in verse 31. The bitterness and wrath of the sinful heart is replaced by the tender forgiveness of the Spirit of Christ.

The disposition of the Christian should discourage harshness and anger. The child of God should be slow to take a brother to task for a fault. He should be quick to overlook it and give the offender another chance.

The Christian does not limit his kindness to those

on his own social level. He is helpful to the unfortunate. He does not allow any class or racial barriers to keep him from ministering to those in need. He is even kind to those who are unkind to him.

Many unbelievers are hardhearted. They are not touched by the needs of others. Not so with God's child. He is like the good Samaritan. He considers everyone in need to be his neighbor. He seeks to do, not the least possible, but the most, when it comes to helping others. He tries to go "the second mile."

Our world is full of sorrow and suffering. God's people should be the ministers of kindness and love. There are discouraged, depressed people all around us who need uplifting.

In this passage Paul speaks especially of others in the Church. How many would have fallen long ago if it had not been for the encouragement of a fellow Christian. We need to exercise a ministry of encouragement as never before. There is enough to discourage us in the world without finding stumbling blocks in our dealings with other Christians.

As long as we are in the flesh there will be offenses even among Christians. But we must not hold grudges against each other. Hard feelings must be quickly put away. We expect others to forgive us, and we should be just as quick to forgive them. A part of the Lord's Prayer is that God will "forgive us our debts, as we forgive our debtors" (Matthew 6:12).

Everything about the disposition of a Christian is to be a refreshing contrast to that found among people of the world. It isn't hard if we let Christ shine out of our lives daily.

10
Stay Out of the Dark

Does any Christian have to be told his surroundings are bad? He may not be imprisoned or tortured, but he will feel the world's hot breath on his neck. A real child of God will be in never-ending collision with hostile spiritual forces. This battle will rage even more fiercely as the time draws closer to the Lord's return. The pressure on the Christian to yield to the spirit of the age will be intense as the age draws to its close.

Dark times for the Church are nothing new. There have been times when it has struggled for its very existence. Our battle today is even more subtle than if we were physically abused. Satan is out to weaken our faith. He tries to destroy our determination and our courage. His aim is to exhaust us spiritually until we stop fighting.

It has never been easy to be a Christian. The Bible doesn't promise that it will be. But victory is always certain if we follow the Lord closely. We must never think in terms of defeat. The goal of victory must be kept before our eyes every day.

NEW OBLIGATIONS

"Be ye therefore followers of God, as dear children; and walk in love, as Christ also hath loved us, and hath given himself for us an offering and a sacrifice to God for a sweetsmelling savor" (Ephesians 5:1, 2).

The Christian has new obligations. He has entered into a new life. He has exchanged bitterness and hatred for love. He has exchanged the image of the world for the image of the Saviour.

In a human family there is a resemblance among the various members. There must be a family likeness in the spiritual realm, too. We must be like Jesus. The believer is called on to be an imitator of God. You may have heard someone say, "That young man looks just like his father." Let's conduct ourselves in such a way that the world will see our Heavenly Father in us!

"Walk in love," Paul commands. There is little love among the worldly. But love among Christians is one of the things the world has always noticed most. It is a clear indication that we have passed from death to life.

Christ's love for us is our great pattern. His love was self-sacrificing. He did not put His own interests first. Always He was concerned about those He came to redeem.

"As Becometh Saints"

"But fornication, and all uncleanness, or covetousness, let it not be once named among you, as becometh saints; neither filthiness, nor foolish talking, nor jesting, which are not convenient: but rather giving of thanks. For this ye know, that no whoremonger, nor unclean person, nor covetous man, who is an idolater, hath any inheritance in the kingdom of Christ and of God. Let no man deceive you with vain words: for because of these things

87

cometh the wrath of God upon the children of disobedience. Be not ye therefore partakers with them" (Ephesians 5:3-7).

It is no accident that Paul's writings have frequent warnings against the sins of immorality. This kind of sin was common then, and in many places it was a part of heathen worship. Paul recognized it as an evil that would destroy spirituality quickly. He knew it would bring the wrath of God upon the individual engaging in it. Human nature has not changed. This is still one of the most widespread of all sins.

Of course, there are other sins against which we must also guard. With one wide sweep Paul cautions vigilance against "all uncleanness." He makes no allowance for indulging in "a little sin." All of it must be shunned. It is not becoming to saints, he declares. God's people are called to be saints (holy ones).

The apostle links the sins of covetousness and greed with the vile and sensual sins. Basically they have the same root. They stem from a refusal to put a bridle on the desires of the ego. All sin represents a determination on man's part to live without any restraint. The sinful nature wants to be held in by no law except its own will.

Words are important too, Paul says. The language of the Christian must be kept clean. Even a lot of small talk that may seem innocent on the surface can lead to conversation that is completely unwholesome.

Let us always ask ourselves when confronted with a decision about a certain course, "Is this becoming to a saint? Will it affect my testimony for Christ in any way?" Usually it isn't hard to know the answer.

Why did Paul have to warn us not to be deceived with "vain words"? Because there have always been false teachers who pretend to be religious but who actually try to destroy all standards of righteousness. They abound today. Their words are "vain," which means "empty." They are clever talkers, but underneath are hearts of deceit. They are tools of Satan. Every New Testament writer spoke of such charlatans.

LIGHT FROM HEAVEN

"For ye were sometime darkness, but now are ye light in the Lord: walk as children of light; (for the fruit of the Spirit is in all goodness and righteousness and truth;) proving what is acceptable unto the Lord. And have no fellowship with the unfruitful works of darkness, but rather reprove them. For it is a shame even to speak of those things which are done of them in secret. But all things that are reproved are made manifest by the light: for whatsoever doth make manifest is light. Wherefore he saith, Awake thou that sleepest, and arise from the dead, and Christ shall give thee light" (Ephesians 5:8-14).

The Christian's light does not have a human origin. It comes from the Lord himself. What a contrast there is between light and darkness. The expression "sometime darkness" describes the past life of sin so well. Thank God, it is different now. The believer has stepped out of the darkness that once overwhelmed his whole being. He has come out into the light that radiates from Christ himself.

Several truths are suggested by the figure of darkness. First, there is fear. The life of sin begets fear. There are so many things to be afraid of if we do not know the Lord. Deliverance from these fears is one of the glorious results of salvation. Darkness also speaks of gloom and depression, while light is the symbol of joy.

There is danger in darkness. Enemies use the night for their deeds of violence. We are apt to stumble when we walk in the dark; we may fall. We can easily take the wrong road. But salvation brings a radical change in the heart and mind. A converted heart means an enlightened understanding. When we were in sin the light was a source of torment. We did not want to be close to it. But now it is a comfort.

Walking in the light causes spiritual fruit to appear in our lives. Paul calls the Spirit's fruit "goodness and righteousness and truth." There was none of this when we were in darkness.

The works of those who walk in darkness are so vile that it embarrasses a good person even to mention them. But the life of a Christian is an open book. His conscience is clear and clean in the sight of God. He is not ashamed to have the world examine his conduct.

Paul introduces what some might call a negative line of teaching when he calls on Christians to have no fellowship with these works of darkness. There are negative aspects to the life of holiness and there is no reason to apologize for them. We must never become so "tolerant" that anything goes!

Don't Be a Fool

"See then that ye walk circumspectly, not as fools, but as wise" (Ephesians 5:15).

All eyes are on the Christian. He cannot afford to deviate from the right path. He must examine every road he takes. He must assure himself that Satan has not hidden any of his booby traps somewhere on the path he is traveling.

We are commanded in Galatians 5:16: "Walk in the Spirit, and ye shall not fulfill the lust of the flesh." The *New American Standard Version* words it this way: "But I say, walk by the Spirit, and you will not carry out the desire of the flesh."

The term *walk* is used often in the Bible. It is a common scriptural expression for the Christian way of life. After all, that is what life is most of the time—a walk. We do very little running. We go through our days a step at a time. We must make sure that every step is a straight one.

If a pilot makes a slight error in charting his course it will not take him long to be far from where he intended his flight to take him. The farther he flies the worse the error becomes. One degree of error in the compass reading can eventually lead the plane hundreds of miles off course.

The same is true spiritually. If we compromise a little in our Christian convictions we will soon get far away from God. One of the ministries of the Holy Spirit is to correct us when He sees us veering off course. May we never ignore His warnings!

The Word of God is a true guide if we will read and follow it faithfully. God has made ample provision to keep us on the right track. If we fail it will be through our own negligence.

Paul urges us to walk *circumspectly*. That means "to look about." The Christian must not walk blindly. He should look around him to make sure he is on the right path.

Paul's words are very strong. He says if we do not walk circumspectly we are fools. Sad to say, this world is full of fools. We must never allow their ideas to influence us. Our convictions must be strong and settled. They must be founded on the Word and constantly impressed upon us afresh by the Holy Spirit.

One of Satan's strategies is to make us worry about being narrow-minded. In our day there is more danger of being too liberal. As God leads us we will find the right balance. The Spirit and the Word will keep us in the middle of the road.

Evil Days

"Redeeming the time, because the days are evil. Wherefore be ye not unwise, but understanding what the will of the Lord is" (Ephesians 5:16, 17).

To redeem the time means literally "buying up the opportunity." Time is a precious thing. It is a gift of God that is not to be wasted.

A steward is one who manages the property of another. The Bible says that Christians are stewards. Sometimes we confine stewardship to the financial realm. But time is another thing we must manage as carefully as money. There are many ways in which men are not equal, but in the matter of time we are all on the same plane. Each one of us has 24 hours in every day.

One of the devil's tricks is to get the Christian occupied in time-consuming things that are of no value. They may not be flagrantly evil, but simply a waste of time. We could settle a good many questions regarding certain practices if we honestly faced the question: "Is it worth the time it will take?"

How fast the days fly past us! Each one is a God-given opportunity. Paul says these opportunities should be bought up. Have you heard someone say, "I don't know where the time goes"? Have you asked a friend to do something in the church, only to get the answer, "I don't have time." Many folks seem to lack time because they do not budget it wisely. They simply waste too much of it.

Frivolous conversation is a great time waster. Many TV and radio programs consume time without actually benefitting the viewer or listener. It is a sad thing for a Christian to sit up so late watching television on Saturday night that he is too sleepy to go to Sunday school!

The reason Paul said we should redeem the time is "because the days are evil." Does anyone need to be convinced of this?

"Be ye not unwise," Paul cautions; meaning literally, "Be not senseless." The unsaved are insensible to the will of God. To the Christian, God's will is the great rule of life. The Holy Spirit, through the Word, gives us constant understanding of that will.

What if those three disciples in Gethsemane had redeemed the time by praying instead of sleeping? Their conduct later that night would have been a different story, wouldn't it have? We must keep ourselves prepared for any test that comes. Who knows what pressure we may be under tomorrow. It will be tragic if we are caught with our guard down because we have failed to use our time to strengthen ourselves spiritually.

THE SINGING CHRISTIAN

"And be not drunk with wine, wherein is excess; but be filled with the Spirit; speaking to yourselves in psalms and hymns and spiritual songs, singing and making melody in your heart to the Lord; giving thanks always for all things unto God and the Father in the name of our Lord Jesus Christ" (Ephesians 5:18-20).

Drunkenness is a work of darkness. It destroys

93

good judgment. Instead of resorting to wine to cheer and stimulate them, Christians are to throw their hearts open to the Holy Spirit. He will fill them and bring a stimulation that is wholesome and good.

The Christian life is not drab. It is overwhelmingly joyful. The apostle refers in this passage not to public worship, but to the believer's private devotional life.

Worship is not cold and lifeless. If it is real it is the most thrilling, vibrant exercise of which a human is capable. The more the Christian sings his hymns of praise the more his soul is lifted up. The Christian life is a glad life. It is full of happiness.

Private worship keeps a Christian's mind in tune with the Lord. The worshiping heart lifts one above the ordinary plane of worldly living. Let's never lose our song!

We must always maintain our spirit of thanksgiving. Otherwise, we are likely to become carnal and careless. When we center our thoughts on things high and holy, suggestions that are evil and impure will be driven out.

There are 150 psalms in the canon of Scripture. This is surely an indication that God wants His people to keep singing. The Book of Psalms was the church's first hymnbook. A few churches still sing psalms instead of conventional hymns. Not everybody has a voice fit for the opera, but if the song comes from the heart it is pleasing to the Lord.

"Giving thanks always." That's a good rule to live by. A thankful spirit is good for our whole being. Every day should be thanksgiving day for God's child. Thanks is to be given "for all things," the apostle declares. This is because God works all things together for good in the lives of His children.

"Submitting yourselves one to another in the fear of God" (Ephesians 5:21).

There is an interdependence among Christians. No one lives or dies to himself. We are involved in a chain of influence. We are influencing someone, and someone is influencing us.

Our church life constantly involves relationships with other people. For the governing of the church there must be some in authority. This means that some must be subordinate. Much damage has been done to God's work because someone has allowed his carnal nature to rebel against submitting himself to God's ordained authority.

Among God's people there is to be a mutual recognition of one another's rights. There are no "big shots" and "little shots" in the Church. Those who govern are to do so in the fear of God. Those who submit are to maintain the same Spirit.

When strife and division are seen among Christians it is an indication that the fear of the Lord has departed from some. It is tragic when God's people are not afraid to promote divisions in the church. Surely there will be a reckoning day for such flagrant violations of God's Word.

11
One Flesh

Marriage bonds are sacred because they are ordained of God. The marriage relationship is an earthly picture of the Church's union with Christ.

Christianity has always exalted marriage and surrounded it with an atmosphere of holiness. The gospel has lifted womanhood from the low plane of the heathen world to her proper place in the plan of God. In marriage the Bible teaches that the wife is her husband's partner, not a piece of property he owns.

The home is the foundation of all society. As our homes go, so go the nation, the world, and every area of human activity. Today's alarming breakup of homes is devastating the whole fabric of our civilization. The majority of juvenile delinquents come from broken homes. Divorce raises more problems than it solves. It is one of the most monstrous evils of our time.

Probably one reason many marriages fail is that they are not on a Christian foundation. The people entering into such marriages do not have the proper understanding of true marriage. Some consider it a trial proposition. This is not the teaching of the Bible. Everything in Scripture is completely contrary to such a distorted notion.

"Wives, submit yourselves unto your own husbands, as unto the Lord. For the husband is the head of the wife, even as Christ is the head of the church: and he is the saviour of the body. Therefore as the church is subject unto Christ, so let the wives be to their own husbands in every thing" (Ephesians 5:22-24).

Christianity beautifies and elevates all relationships of life. Christians should be better husbands and wives than non-Christians. A Christian home should be a little corner of heaven on earth.

Paul was not one-sided in his views. He talks about the duties of both husbands and wives. One cannot make a success of marriage alone. It takes the cooperation of both partners.

Although Christianity emancipates and elevates womanhood, it does not release woman from the duty of subjection to her husband. God has made the husband the head of the home.

The woman was made for man in the beginning (Genesis 2:18), even as the Church was made for Christ. As Christ is the Head of the Church, so man is the head of the home.

It is apparent in Paul's thinking that the wife's subjection to her husband does not come ahead of her subjection to Christ. In the life of the wife there are three wills involved: God's, her husband's, and her own. If there is any conflict among these, the order of consideration is the same—God's will first, her husband's second, and hers last.

When a marriage truly succeeds it is because both parties work to make it so. When a marriage fails, someone has neglected to live up to his or her part of

97

the bargain. Sometimes both are at fault. Marriage is what both husband and wife are willing to make it.

Man was created first. On his shoulders rests the responsibility of being the leader of the household. Some have objected to the word *obey* in the wife's part of the wedding ceremony. There is a resentment on the part of some toward the subjection of the wife to her husband. But we must safeguard this scriptural relationship and not try to change God's perfect plan.

This subjection is not servitude, however. The gospel lifts the wife above the level of the household slave—far, far above it. The wife's subjection is a submission that recognizes her husband's rule as just, tender, and wise. It is a loving obedience, and of course one that has its limitations, for the wife's obedience to her husband does not supersede her fidelity to the Lord.

THE HOMEMAKER

In this lesson we have an insight into what Christ has done for the family. He has made marriage the symbol of His own relationship to the Church. Thus, the whole life of the family is exalted in a way that the unspiritual mind fails to comprehend.

The wife's subjection to her husband does not imply that he is superior to her in every respect. It does imply that he is superior in those areas that fit him to be the head of the home. His physical strength and self-reliance make him the natural leader. He must stand between his wife and the world. He must shield her from harm. While she keeps the home he goes out to earn the living. Hence it is fitting that she should lean upon him and be guided by him.

Woman was made with a natural love for her home

and family. The instincts of motherhood develop early within her consciousness. Of all the achievements of women none is greater than that of being a good homemaker, a good wife, and a good mother.

It is one of the tragedies of our time that rising prices and economic pressure on the family have forced so many wives and mothers to seek employment to supplement the family income. Undoubtedly this has put a great strain on many marriages. While it is a situation that must be tolerated out of necessity in some cases, it certainly is not the ideal. It is worth sacrificing a few luxuries for the wife to be in her place, the home.

Great changes have taken place in our society in recent years. Women have entered the fields of business and industry as never before. We have even had women in the cabinets of some presidents. Undoubtedly many women have made valuable contributions in many areas.

But it is tragic when women try to be like men. Some have foolishly imagined that to achieve equality they must drink, smoke, and curse like men, throw their morals to the winds, and in other frivolous ways try to capture the attention of the male sex. The fact is that men still love femininity in women. The wife who would please her husband will do well to stay gentle, sweet, gracious, and ladylike. In the long run this will pay great dividends. And it will strengthen the marriage and home.

Give Ear, You Husbands!

"Husbands, love your wives, even as Christ also loved the church, and gave himself for it; that he might sanctify and cleanse it with the washing of water by the word, that he might present it to himself a glorious church, not having spot, or wrinkle, or any such thing; but that it should be holy and without blemish. So ought men to love their wives as their own bodies. He that loveth his wife loveth himself" (Ephesians 5:25-28).

There is no room in Christian marriage for an overbearing, cruel domination by the husband. He is to rule with love, even as Christ rules the Church with love.

Our Saviour's example of self-sacrifice is held up to all husbands as their model. Jesus loved the Church enough to give His life for it. Husbands are to have the same attitude toward their wives. It is not hard for a wife to be in subjection to a husband who displays such a spirit.

Christ's loving heart always seeks the Church's highest good. So should the husband be mindful of his wife's highest interests, and not merely of his own pleasure. Everything Christ does for His bride, the Church, is for her edification and advancement.

The Church reaches its completeness as it becomes one with Christ. So does the woman achieve her completeness by her union with her husband. When Jesus comes again it will be a day of great joy for Him as well as for the Church. The joy of that day is foreshadowed in the happiness surrounding the wedding ceremony on earth.

A man's wife is so much a part of him that if he does not love her it is as though he does not love himself. This, of course, is completely unnatural.

Christ does not merely pity the Church; He loves it. The Church's image is stamped on His heart. This kind of love, says Paul, should characterize the husband's feeling toward his wife. The rule of the husband must not be that of a dictator. Who could imagine Christ "bullying" the Church? Our Lord's governing of His church is in tenderness and love. The husband is to follow this example in his home.

The duty of the wife is bound up in the single duty of subjection. The duty of the husband is comprehended in the single duty of love. If these qualities are present, everything else will fall into its natural place. If either or both is lacking, the marriage is certain to labor under a handicap. How wise we are to follow God's way rather than man's.

It's a Big Job, Men!

The husband's love for his wife is to be single, exclusive, and undivided. He is to love her and no other. There are those who foolishly cling to what has been called a "double standard." This means that the wife should be faithful but that it is all right for the husband to "play around." Nothing could be farther from the teaching of Scripture. The husband is as obligated to be faithful as his wife.

Some men may consider it amusing to flirt. They excuse themselves by calling it an innocent pastime. But such a practice can never be truly innocent. Anything that takes a husband's affection for one moment from his wife is wrong.

The husband must be considerate and tender. The wife is to be given due consideration as "the weaker vessel." The husband's love for her should be constant and lasting, regardless of the weaknesses and failings she may have. (He should remember his own!)

It should go without saying that it is the husband's duty to provide for the financial support of his wife. In 1 Timothy 5:8 Paul says, "If any provide not for his own, and specially for those of his own house, he

hath denied the faith, and is worse than an infidel."
There is nothing more contemptible than a lazy husband who refuses to make a living for his family.

The husband must consider his wife's happiness and pleasure. He must protect her life, her honor, and her good name. He is to seek her spiritual welfare, praying for her and with her. He must realize that they are "heirs together of the grace of life" (1 Peter 3:7). How true it is that the family that prays together stays together.

Some men might shrink from showing love and affection to their wives because they think it makes them look weak. Such reasoning certainly is not true. Paul says that when a man loves his wife he is loving himself, since they are one.

In this passage we have God's picture of a true husband. He rules, but he does it by love, not force. It is a distorted idea to imagine that a man must be rough and harsh to be a real husband. This is not in keeping with the Bible.

There should be mutual sympathy between husbands and wives. There should also be mutual confidence. Never must a breakdown of communication be allowed to develop. The basis of true love is trust. And both partners must work at this. To have such trust in a marriage is certainly worth all the effort.

Not Two, But One

"For we are members of his body, of his flesh, and of his bones. For this cause shall a man leave his father and mother, and shall be joined unto his wife, and they two shall be one flesh. This is a great mystery: but I speak concerning Christ and the church. Nevertheless, let every one of you in particular so love his wife even as himself; and the wife see that

102

she reverence her husband" (Ephesians 5:30-33).

No other passage of Scripture sets forth so emphatically the closeness between Christ and His people.

Salvation is more than the acceptance of a creed. It is a vital, living union between the Saviour and the believer. This union was foreshadowed in the creation of Eve. As a type of the Church she was taken out of Adam, a type of Christ.

When God created the first couple He commanded that they should be one flesh. Upon this principle the Bible opposes divorce.

Despite modern misconceptions, God's divine order for marriage is still this: One man for one woman for life! No one should approach the marriage altar with any other thought in mind. That bond lasts "until death do us part"!

Our easy divorce laws are one of the great curses our nation has brought on itself. Jesus made it clear that only adultery gives people grounds for divorce (Matthew 19:9). However, if the offended party can find it possible to forgive it is better not to divorce even when adultery has been committed. There have been instances where the guilty partner has repented and reformed, and the home has been saved. Certainly it takes considerable grace and forbearance on the part of the other companion to endure such a trial. But God will grant such grace, for He is mightily concerned with the saving of the home.

It has been well said that an ounce of prevention is worth a pound of cure. If those contemplating marriage would realize its sacredness ahead of time and consider the step more prayerfully and carefully much harm could be avoided.

Too many rush headlong into marriage without

considering the background of the other person and his or her other qualifications. Some "whirlwind courtships" do not allow sufficient time to find out if the two are really suited to each other.

It is tragic that there are so many pressures on young people today to marry. No doubt many have thought of matrimony as a "must" because everyone else seems to be getting married and it is the "in" thing.

THESE BONDS ARE SACRED

Undoubtedly many have mistaken infatuation for love. There is a real need for renewed emphasis on the permanence of marriage. Those who take this serious step should do so with a very sober mind.

A Christian cannot help feeling sad at a wedding that is celebrated with alcohol and frivolous revelry. Marriage is an occasion for joy, but it should be tempered with reverence and sobriety. When two people repeat the marriage vows they are entering into the most sacred of all human relationships. It is one ordained by God himself. It is His doing, not man's.

In Matthew 19 the Pharisees were arguing with Jesus about divorce. They asked Him if a man might divorce his wife for every cause. Jesus went back to the very beginning to enunciate the divine standard of marriage: "Have ye not read, that he which made them at the beginning made them male and female, and said, For this cause shall a man leave father and mother, and shall cleave to his wife: and they twain shall be one flesh? Wherefore they are no more twain, but one flesh. What therefore God hath joined together, let not man put asunder" (Matthew 19:4-6).

Thus the Creator himself ordained the permanence of the marriage bonds. Man breaks this law at his own peril. Divorce leaves a mark on the parties involved that never completely disappears. No one can live with another as husband or wife and then forget it in a moment just because a judge signs a piece of paper. It is not that simple!

What about couples who are not compatible? Certainly they should think of their children and try at all costs to save the home for their sakes. The average child will suffer terrible emotional upset if his parents are divorced. He may be attached to one more than the other, but he still loves both. How tragic for him to be torn between two loyalties.

As great as our loyalty to our parents should be, the Bible teaches that faithfulness to one's husband or wife comes ahead of even the love to father or mother. That's how holy those marriage bonds are!

12
You Can't Escape Your Duty

Paul was intensely practical. In Ephesians he soars into the heavenlies. But before he finishes he is back down on earth telling us how to live our everyday Christian lives.

Christians are in this present world. There's no way to run away from it. Until the Lord calls us home we have to cope with human problems. We have to live with other people, good and bad.

Being a Christian does not free us from our obligations to others. On the contrary, it intensifies those obligations. The believer is an example. He is being watched. He lives his life in a goldfish bowl, so to speak. Someone may be saved or lost by the way a Christian conducts himself.

Our whole society badly needs Christian influence. The home needs it. The business world needs it. So does our educational system. Christianity must be practiced unceasingly. It is a life to be lived, not just a creed to be believed. Someone has said, "I'd rather see a sermon than hear one any day." And haven't you heard, "Your actions speak so loud that I can't hear a word you say"?

This doesn't mean a Christian has to be a hermit. Jesus lived and walked among men. But instead of their dragging Him down He lifted them up. This is how it should be with all of us who are His disciples. We can't be isolationists. While rubbing shoulders with the world we must conduct ourselves according to the will of God. We must maintain right relationships with others. We must serve God in the home, in the community, and in business.

It is tragic to hear anyone complain, "I can't live the Christian life where I work," or "where I live," or "where I go to school." This is denying the power of Christ. He has promised to keep us wherever we are. This defeatist attitude betrays a lack of "want to." God does the keeping, but we must want to be kept.

There should be a refinement about a Christian that stands out in contrast to his worldly surroundings. A Christian should always be a perfect gentleman; a perfect lady. We should influence the atmosphere around us instead of its influencing us. Our neighborhoods, our homes, our places of employment, should be better for our having been there. We are not trying to call attention to ourselves, but to our Lord. Our goal is that men shall see our good works and glorify our Heavenly Father.

LISTEN, KIDS!

Children, obey your parents in the Lord: for this is right. Honor thy father and mother; which is the first commandment with promise; that it may be well with thee, and thou mayest live long on the earth" (Ephesians 6:1-3).

There are some things we should do simply because they are right. This is the basis for the admonition to obey our parents. "It is right," Paul declares. No further explanation is needed.

Many books have been written on the raising of

107

children. Very few, if any, are written to tell children how to treat their parents. Sons and daughters must bear their share of the responsibility; otherwise, there will not be peace and harmony in the home.

The breakdown of the American home is devastating our society. One of the worst features of this collapse is the disrespect many children show their parents. In many instances there is downright rebellion. Sometimes there is actual hatred. Satan is the author of this. Such a spirit must be kept far from the homes of Christians. Our nation is paying dearly for this deterioration of our homes.

Certainly no child can be a true Christian and be consistently willful, disrespectful, and disobedient. The spirit of lawlessness is the spirit of Satan. The Christlike spirit is submissive, tender, and gentle. The arrogant one considers nobody's will but his own. The one who follows Jesus is very thoughtful of others.

Paul does not spend time arguing about the obedience of children. For our cynical age doing something because it is right may not be a sufficient reason. But this is Biblical, nevertheless. Paul also says that obedience to parents is a commandment. It is something binding because it is from the Lord. Children are not to love their parents more than they love God, but they are to love them "in the Lord." Love for one's parents will certainly enhance love for God.

Parents occupy a remarkable place in God's plan. As God was the Giver of life in the beginning, so parents, under God, are the givers of life to their children. This makes parenthood a very sacred thing. And it underscores the importance of obedience to those parents.

Children are always under pressure from their peers. But they must not feel they can disregard their parents' wishes because others do. Some young people like to brag about "putting it over" on dad and mom. The Christian will refuse to be influenced by such talk.

THE WORLD'S BIGGEST JOB—PARENTHOOD

"And, ye fathers, provoke not your children to wrath: but bring them up in the nurture and admonition of the Lord" (Ephesians 6:4).

In Paul's day some parents may have been too severe, just as some are now too lenient. The apostle reminds parents that discipline is to be administered in love. He addresses the father because he is the head of the household, but of course the instructions include both parents.

There are two sides to the matter of discipline. The child is to show obedience and respect. The parents are also obligated to use common sense and good judgment. Especially are they to avoid temper tantrums of their own that would be a source of irritation and vexation to their children.

Children are to be regarded as a gift from God. Parents must consider raising them as a sacred responsibility. In addition to providing for them they must also teach them the ways of righteousness. With Christians, the ruthless command is replaced by the understanding heart. There is a difference between hardness and firmness. But surely the Scripture teaches that there is to be government in the home. There must be discipline and an exercising of authority.

One of our great problems today is juvenile delinquency. Often it can be traced to a lack of discipline in the home. Children are allowed to do "their own thing" with no parental restraint. This is not wholesome. It does not show love, but a lack of it. Even when children are rebellious they are often longing for the parents to say "No!"

Too many parents want to get rid of their children any way they can. They do not care where they are as long as they are out from under their feet. Teenagers turned loose with high-powered automobiles, plenty of spending money, and no supervision are headed for nothing but trouble. They will become the kind of adults who will make their parents anything but happy.

When parents fail to exercise discipline in the home they are taking the path of least resistance. It is much easier to turn one's head and ignore a situation in which punishment is deserved than to administer the needed discipline. But it is far better for parents to stop the wrongdoing of their children than for the police to have to do it.

Surely God will give parents the needed wisdom, patience, and grace if they will be prayerful about their responsibilities. Who ever said that being a father or mother is easy?

"The Nurture and Admonition of the Lord"

A Christian home should be a little heaven on this earth. What wonderful homes we would have if all parents followed the admonition to bring their children up "in the nurture and admonition of the Lord."

All too often religious instruction is missing even in Christian households. All week long our boys and girls are exposed to the influence of the world. They spend a large part of their day in the schoolroom. After classes they are with friends, watching TV, reading magazines, or playing games. What a small amount of time is left for the vital matter of taking care of their spiritual needs. We have our children with us such a short time, and we need to make every moment count. After all, we are dealing with immortal souls.

Nurture means education and training. This includes discipline and correction. *Admonition* means "calling attention to." It implies rebukes and warnings. God sometimes rebukes us, and we are failing if we do not do the same with our children when it is needed. "Nurture" could be accurately translated "training." Spiritual training is a never-ending job. It takes skill, patience, and devotion. It involves both rewards and punishment for the trainee. It takes more than human wisdom to know which one is needed in each circumstance!

Both the nurture and admonition are to be "of the Lord." It is the kind that He inspires and approves. The Christian parent must instill sound principles of living. He must set the example of good habits. He must caution and protect against moral dangers. It is necessary for him to encourage prayer, Bible reading, and church attendance. The Christian parent must carefully oversee the company his children keep. Above all he should lead them into a personal experience with Christ as early as possible. Let no one imagine this can be put off until the child is well advanced in age. Children are ready to accept Christ very early in life, and those precious years should not be allowed to slip by without such a decision.

Christian parents are bucking a strong tide today, but God will give grace to those who are determined to raise their children the Biblical way. We must not surrender to the spirit of the age. Don't cry, "It's no use." Pray and try. Then pray and try some more.

Certainly we should supervise our children's reading material and TV watching, and we should introduce them to good, wholesome music.

CHRISTIANS ON THE JOB

"Servants, be obedient to them that are your masters according to the flesh, with fear and trembling, in singleness of your heart, as unto Christ; not with eyeservice, as menpleasers; but as the servants of Christ, doing the will of God from the heart; with good will doing service, as to the Lord, and not to men: knowing that whatsoever good thing any man doeth, the same shall he receive of the Lord, whether he be bond or free" (Ephesians 6:5-8).

There were many slaves in the Early Church. But even though their position may have seemed unjust to them the apostle could not advise them to be disobedient or disloyal. As Christians they must be faithful and conscientious. Such a course would more likely result in their emancipation.

The expression "with fear and trembling" does not indicate that servants should be filled with morbid dread. It simply means they should be constantly on guard to see that they do not fail in their duty. Even though it might be irksome to be in slavery, their experience would be sweetened if they considered what they were doing as working for Christ.

Thank God, slavery has been abolished. But we still have employers and employees. The principles Paul sets forth here are applicable for Christian employees today. It is possible for one to perform a good service in an outward and formal manner. Christians are to render their service from the heart.

112

The Christian employee should be full of good will, not hatred, toward those placed over him.

An employee owes it to the one who hires him and pays his salary to work for the best interests of the firm at all times. It is not the Spirit of Christ to reason, "I'm going to give them as little as possible for the pay I receive." The Christian goes the "second mile." He will not steal his employer's time any more than his money. He will not take advantage of his employer's goodness.

What if the boss is a tyrant? The Christian, by his example, must be a witness for Christ. God will give grace under disagreeable circumstances. God's man must not be unkind to the one who is hard to get along with. He might even win that hard-boiled boss to the Lord. It is certain that he will not help himself by constantly fretting over the situation.

"UNTO CHRIST"

We should consider everything we do as done "unto Christ." If the Christian must bear some unpleasant things in connection with his job he should consider that he is doing it for the Lord's sake. If he misses a promotion because he will not compromise his convictions he should rest in the assurance that he is suffering for the Lord's sake. He should do everything he can to make himself a better employee, not only for the benefit of his company, but also because it is a good testimony for his Saviour.

A Christian should maintain a cheerful attitude toward his work. It is a poor example for a child of God to be forever grumbling. He must not fight back against those who are ill-tempered and sarcastic.

Under such conditions he should remain sweet and Christlike.

As long as we are in this world we must work. God has decreed it so. We would not be happy doing otherwise. Let the child of the Lord go about his business with diligence. Let him do every job "with good will doing service, as to the Lord, and not to men." If he is not always rewarded here certainly he will be in the life to come. Actually, the knowledge that you have done your best is a reward in itself. It gives you a clear conscience, too.

BE A GOOD BOSS!

"And, ye masters, do the same things unto them, forbearing threatening: knowing that your Master also is in heaven; neither is there respect of persons with him" (Ephesians 6:9).

Sometimes the Christian is in the position of employer. As such he has the responsibility of maintaining the right kind of standards in relation to his employees. It is a poor Christian who does not have a good testimony among those who work for him.

In this verse Paul reminds masters that there is a Master over them. They must be ever mindful of His authority. The Christian employer should recognize that there is one above him to whom he must one day give account.

Paul, of course, was talking to masters about their slaves. He did not command them to release the slaves. This was an evil that Paul knew could not be eliminated overnight. But as long as a Christian had slaves he was to act as though the eye of the Lord was constantly upon him in his actions toward them. This basic principle applies to those who supervise others in today's workaday world.

A Christian employer must always be a man of his word. He must avoid favoritism. It is not necessary for him to overpay his workers, but neither must he try to get as much out of them as he can for as little pay as possible.

Paul cautions the masters of slaves against grinding them down, defrauding them, scolding them unreasonably, and making their lives miserable. Doubtless he would say the same thing to anyone who employs others. If the employee is to do service as unto the Lord the employer must be Christlike in his requirements of service. While a boss must be firm, he, as a child of God, should not habitually display a bad temper or sour disposition. He will likely not win his workers to Christ if he does.

If God has allowed one of His children to be promoted and achieve a place of high standing in the business world, surely responsibility goes along with the blessing. Regardless of his position he is first a Christian. It would be fatal to his testimony to be unchristian in any of his business practices.

Some businessmen may think they must sell liquor or beer in their stores. Others may feel they will go bankrupt if they do not stay open on Sundays. Yet if we will put God's business first He will take care of ours. If compromise is made in one direction it will be easy to make it in another.

13

No Room for Faint Hearts

In case you hadn't noticed, the Christian life is a battlefield. It takes tough people to live for God. It's not for weak spines and faint hearts. Every believer is a soldier whether he likes it or not.

There is in this universe an evil supernatural personality. His name is Satan. He is opposed to God and righteousness. This means he is opposed to anyone who tries to obey God. Satan is out to defeat God's plan. Christians are a part of that plan, so he is after us.

A smart general will not use the same tactics all the time. He will suit his strategy to the occasion. Satan is this kind of general. He uses a variety of schemes. He is cunning, vicious, fierce, and determined.

But never for a moment should we allow an attitude of defeat to take over our spirits. God has provided spiritual equipment for our victory. That's what Paul talks about in Ephesians 6.

Our adversary is strong, but we can beat him if we will use God's weapons. Since armor, swords, spears, and shields were used in Paul's day these are what he uses as illustrations. In his description of our spiritual armor nothing is said about the back. No protection is given for that part of us. The Lord never intends for His army to retreat. It must always be on the advance.

The Christian must think in terms of victory. He cannot make it by his own strength or cleverness. But in the strength of the Lord he can come out on top instead of on the bottom. He may get a few scars, but he will be on the winning side.

Determination is probably one of the greatest qualities God's people must develop. We must be as tenacious as bulldogs. We must never say "die." If we aren't too sure we want to stand up and fight we will soon be driven from the battlefield in defeat.

Never underestimate the power of your enemy. Don't think about Satan so much that you become morbid, but don't take him lightly either. Never let your guard down. Satan is circling every Christian moment by moment, looking for that weak spot where he can strike a telling blow.

God has promised to renew our strength daily. This comes through prayer and the study of the Word. It comes through worship and Christian fellowship. Let us never neglect these means of grace.

THE WHOLE ARMOR

"Finally, my brethren, be strong in the Lord, and in the power of his might. Put on the whole armor of God, . . . that ye may be able to withstand in the evil day, and having done all, to stand" (Ephesians 6:10, 11, 13).

The first part of this passage means literally, "Be made powerful in the Lord, and in the strength of His might." We don't become spiritually powerful by being lackadaisical. There must be determined perseverance. Diligent study of the Word is required,

117

along with a consistent prayer life. Never has wishful thinking produced spiritual power.

Our strength is "in the Lord." It comes by the constant indwelling of the Holy Spirit. Faith is the lifeline that keeps this strength flowing.

The life of a soldier is one of discipline. God does not put the armor on us. We must put it on ourselves. It is to be the *whole* armor. No part can be left off. Every area of our life needs protection. Our spiritual enemies are many. We need the right weapons for all of them.

The Christian's warfare is against more than the natural tendencies of his flesh. There are forces in the unseen world of spirits against which we would be helpless if left to ourselves. These vicious beings are continually warring against believers. They try to molest and trouble them without letup.

Note the two words *withstand* and *stand*. The Christian must do both. To withstand is to resist, to fight back vigorously. The Christian cannot be passive. He must wage his battle with all his heart. He must pray fervently. He must keep his Bible in his hand. He dare not neglect his church attendance. He must witness. When temptation suddenly looms in front of him he must resist it with no thought of surrender.

The Christian does not keep moving backward. He stands. He keeps erect and upright. He never turns his back on the enemy.

Paul refers to "the evil day." Such a time comes in one way or another to all Christians. It may be a season of severe temptation. It may take the form of financial loss. It may come through bereavement, when we feel alone and forsaken. In such an hour we must call upon the Lord for His strength. Then we will stand and not fall.

"Having done all," Paul says. Have we done our best? Have we really tried? Have we put forth the maximum effort? If so, we can rest in the Lord and know that He will stand beside us in the conflict.

An Enemy You Can't See or Touch

"That ye may be able to stand against the wiles of the devil. For we wrestle not against flesh and blood, but against principalities, against powers, against the rulers of the darkness of this world, against spiritual wickedness in high places" (Ephesians 6:11, 12).

The fact that our enemy is unseen does not make him less real. When we were in sin we were guided by the forces of Satan. Once we are saved we find ourselves in conflict with these forces. They are bent on our destruction.

Let no one doubt that these evil spirits are personal. The devil is a spirit, but he is an actual being. So are demons. These evil spirits hinder us in our prayers. They bring mental oppression and feelings of discouragement. They slip evil thoughts into our minds. They will leave no stone unturned to come between the Christian and his Lord.

Peter says the devil is a roaring lion seeking his prey (1 Peter 5:8). He is an accuser (Revelation 12:10) and a tempter (1 Thessalonians 3:5). In the Parable of the Sower Jesus pictured Satan as the one who steals the Word out of the heart (Mark 4:15). It was Satan who influenced Judas to betray Jesus (John 13:2). And he put it into the heart of Ananias and Sapphira to lie to the Holy Ghost (Acts 5:3).

In Ephesians 2:2 Paul calls Satan "the spirit that

now worketh in the children of disobedience."
Think about that for a moment. It shows that the
devil's influence over sinners is not passive, but
intensely active.

In 2 Corinthians 4:4 Satan is named "the god of
this world." This means he is in control of the minds
and hearts of people outside of Christ. Paul warns
Christians to be on guard "lest Satan should get an
advantage of us" (2 Corinthians 2:11).

Satan never shows his true face. He masquerades
an an angel of light (2 Corinthians 11:14). He makes
sin attractive. Jesus taught the disciples to pray, "Deliver us from evil." This means literally, "Deliver us
from the evil one." That, of course, means Satan.

Wrestling is close-range combat. The opponents
are eyeball to eyeball. They have hold of each other.
It is a very personal struggle. Each one feels the
other's hot breath. This is the way Paul describes the
Christian's fight. No wonder he calls for strength and
courage. Wrestling against forces that are not physical is the hardest struggle of all.

THE GIRDLE AND BREASTPLATE

"Stand therefore, having your loins girt about with
truth, and having on the breastplate of righteousness" (Ephesians 6:14).

Now Paul begins to name the parts of the Christian's armor. Each one has a spiritual significance.
The soldier who wears all of this equipment is ready
for the battlefield.

The girdle was a belt for the waist which held the
breastplate in place. The girdle is "truth," Paul says.
The Christian must have the truth of the gospel literally wrapped around him. Without the girdle the
soldier could not keep the rest of the armor on. It

actually bound the other parts together. Our faith in the saving truth of the gospel binds together our whole Christian experience.

Some might try to wear the breastplate of righteousness without a genuine born-again experience. This is impossible. It doesn't take long for failure to show itself in such lives. The armor soon falls off. There is nothing to hold it together.

Satan has a hard time with the one whose heart is full of truth. This is why every Christian should be a diligent student of the Word. The eternal truths of the Bible will develop a character which the devil cannot touch. The man whose heart is not full of the truth will have weak convictions—if he has any at all. He will never be sure where he stands. He can easily be driven back.

The breastplate covered the heart. A soldier without a breastplate would probably not live long. It would not take an enemy swordsman long to strike a vital spot. The Christian who does not live a righteous life will likewise be exposing himself to spiritual disaster.

We must heed God's call to holiness; otherwise, we are heading for a crushing defeat. If we become careless and let the world into our hearts we will give Satan an advantage. But if our hearts are covered by the righteousness of Christ the devil has no means of entrance.

The breastplate was probably the heaviest part of the armor. It was more difficult and awkward to put on than the smaller pieces, but it was worth the effort because of the protection it afforded. The effort we make to live righteously will be rewarded by victories in the hardest fights.

"Truth" and "righteousness"—what a powerful

combination. The two go together naturally. There is no way to separate them.

THERE'S A LOT OF WALKING

"And your feet shod with the preparation of the gospel of peace" (Ephesians 6:15).

The Roman infantryman had to do a lot of walking. Consequently, the military sandals he wore were an important part of his equipment. If a soldier can't walk he won't be able to do much fighting.

Frequently the Bible calls the Christian life a "walk." There is nothing glamorous about walking. It just takes a lot of endurance and patience. But that's how we get to heaven—by walking with God day by day.

The infantry has always been the mainstay of the army. There were chariots in the Roman army, but the foot soldier bore the brunt of the battle. Naturally his feet had to be well protected. Sometimes he fought on very rough ground and could not afford to wear shoes that would allow his feet to be bruised.

The Roman military sandal was furnished with nails that gripped the ground firmly. This was especially important if the ground was sloped or slippery. The shoes had a steadying effect on the soldier. They kept him upright and firm. He could walk with confidence regardless of the terrain.

The gospel of peace in the heart is a steadying influence. It keeps one upright even when he does his walking in a corrupt world.

The moral ground of this age is very slippery. Many are falling. But the true Christian soldier is shod with footwear that keeps him going onward and upward. He can stand erect even when life deals him heavy blows. He does not lose his balance when the fighting gets hot.

Sometimes the Roman soldier moved slowly. Sometimes he had to be very swift of foot. But whether he was walking or running he was always prepared. He wore suitable shoes.

In the Christian life our advance is often very slow. But there are times when we seem to move ahead rapidly. In either case our faith in the saving gospel gives us sure footing.

The reference to footwear could also point to the evangelistic effort of the Church. The Christian must "go" with the gospel. He must keep on going and going and going. There is no stopping place. Until the Lord comes or calls us home we must be on the move.

Watch your feet, Christian! The devil is an expert at tripping people—sometimes over something very small. Pay close attention to your walk. Everyone else does! You can't afford to fall.

THE SHIELD, HELMET, AND SWORD

"Above all, taking the shield of faith, wherewith ye shall be able to quench all the fiery darts of the wicked. And take the helmet of salvation, and the sword of the Spirit, which is the word of God" (Ephesians 6:16, 17).

The shield was a defensive weapon. We must take it "above all," Paul says. No soldier could hope to be agile enough to dodge all of the arrows shot at him. He needed a shield that he could throw in front of himself to stop those missiles.

Weak faith will soon render the Christian prey to the enemy's thrusts. We need our shield—it is what defends us against Satan's onslaughts. Paul is not

123

talking about just any kind of faith. The faith that is a real shield is faith in the shed blood of Jesus, in the Word of God, in the Holy Spirit, and in the whole truth of the gospel.

The helmet was the head covering. The glorious truth of our salvation protects our minds from the invading thoughts of the evil one.

Doesn't sin start in the head? Every act is first a thought. This is why the devil aims for the mind. The thought life controls the rest of the life. The Christian must never leave his mind uncovered for the enemy to enter.

When the ancient soldier rushed into battle he had to keep his head up so he could observe his opponents. The helmet enabled him to do this without fear of injury. It is certainly true that our minds are more exposed to satanic influence than any other part of us. That is why we need the covering of the gospel.

The sword was the soldier's offensive weapon. Without it he couldn't kill many enemies. Paul says the Word of God is sharper than a sword with two edges (Hebrews 4:12). The Christian must use the Word in his battle with temptation. When the mind is well stored with Scripture the Holy Spirit will instantly suggest the promise that is needed to meet the attack of the moment. The only weapon Satan fears is the Bible.

The Christian must contend as well as defend. That's why he must keep his sword sharp. Don't let your Bible gather dust! Hide it in your heart. Put some of it there every day. Develop skill in your use of the Scripture. This takes time and much self-discipline, but it's worth it.

It is good to read books about the Bible, but they

can't take the place of the Bible itself. Be a lover of the Word!

THE SECRET WEAPON

"Praying always with all prayer and supplication in the Spirit, and watching thereunto with all perseverance and supplication for all saints; and for me, that utterance may be given unto me, that I may open my mouth boldly, to make known the mystery of the gospel, for which I am an ambassador in bonds; that therein I may speak boldly, as I ought to speak" (Ephesians 6:18-20).

The Christian's secret weapon is the artillery of prayer. The moment he starts praying Satan begins retreating. When we become occupied with God in prayer we are lifted into a realm where the devil can't defeat us.

"IN CLOSING"

"But that ye also may know my affairs, and how I do, Tychicus, a beloved brother and faithful minister in the Lord, shall make known to you all things: whom I have sent unto you for the same purpose, that ye might know our affairs, and that he might comfort your hearts. Peace be to the brethren, and love with faith, from God the Father and the Lord Jesus Christ. Grace be with all them that love our Lord Jesus Christ in sincerity. Amen" (Ephesians 6:21-24).

Thanks, Paul. You've helped us a lot!